Why Buy This Guide?

Ok, this is how I see it. It's really hard to become an expert in cla
sharing your time with 30 other students. I began my YouTube ch
30-minute video would teach my students much more than I coulc
minute lesson. And it's true.

This guide should do the same for you, and make you an expert much more quickly than
you can in school.

These are typical comments I get after the GCSE exams:

Ayesha Khan

Hi Mr Salles,

Thanks to your videos I got two grade nines in English Literature and English Language!
Keep doing what you're doing because you're great at it :)

KM Davies

Thanks for uploading all the brilliant videos. I never thought I'd end up with two 9s in
English! Recommended you to my school :)

Alanna Smith

As a teacher planning for Year 10 literature next year, you are an invaluable resource!
Thank you so much - you don't just help the kids!

Tapster Chitiga

Honestly want to thank you so much, got me from a 6 in my mocks to a 9 in English
language, the guide really was very useful as well as the videos!!

Ellie S

Hey!! I got 9s in both English Literature and Language. I'm over the moon!! Thank you
for your videos!!

Charlotte

Hey, remember me?! Just wanted to let you know that I got an 8 (A*) in English
Literature today and I guess the point of this comment is to say thank you! Without your
videos and analysis on Macbeth and poetry I honestly wouldn't have done as well as I
was expected! From getting consistent B's in mocks to an A* made me beam with
happiness and honestly, I am just so so happy! Now I'm off to do both English's and
Media at A-level! Your videos have helped me tremendously and I just don't know how
to thank you enough! 😊 😊

Riannon Chaplin

I just got a 9 in English Language as early entry, thank you so much for your revision guides and videos - I wouldn't have been able to do it without you :)

Kirsty Barnett

I GOT TWO 9S IN ENGLISH and I honestly can't thank you enough!!! Your videos helped me so much and I wouldn't have done nearly as well without them so I'll NEVER EVER stop recommending them to people. Thank you thank you thank you!

Viewers' Poll

- **40% of my viewers say they went up at least two grades as a result of watching my videos!**
- **Another 40% say they went up one grade.**

Imagine how many grades you'll improve with this full guide? You really can move from grade 4 to grades 8 and 9.

Big Pat on the Back

Ok, big pat on the back for me, and high fives all round! But take another look. Something really important is going on here. They had to watch the videos, which takes some effort. These take time. Many students switch off after 5 or 6 minutes. If that's you, you can probably kiss the grades 7, 8 and 9 goodbye.

But, if you pay attention and put in some time, you really can go from grade 6 to grade 8 or 9. Let's say you spend two hours reading this guide. Then a week later spend another 2 hours making notes from it, testing what you remember. Will you really go up a grade or two grades?

Yes, you will.

Why? Because grade 8 and 9 ideas are hard to come up with. But are they hard to remember? No. It's just memory, it's just knowing stuff.

All you have to do is pay attention to this guide and use some of its ideas to get a better grade.

In this guide you will meet at least **100** ideas that you've never discussed in class. If you use only **5** of these in your exam, your answer will be more advanced than nearly everyone else's in the exam room. Knowing more will simply make you smarter.

If you pay attention, this guide will transform your grade.

Why did Priestley Write <u>An Inspector Calls</u>?

It's 1918. You are 22 years old, and The First World War began when you were 17. Imagine you have fought through this war which has devastated every community in Britain. Imagine you have watched friends killed in a display of horrifying waste, for 5 long years, in the world's greatest war. Imagine nearly one in ten soldiers had been killed.

To put that in context for you, so you can properly imagine it, that's 1 or 2 boys in your tutor group. And every other tutor group in your year. And, because the war lasted 5 years, that's the same in every single tutor group in your school. Now replicate that across all schools in the country, and that's what The First World War took away. In a school of 1000 boys, 100 of them are dead.

Now, imagine you have survived that. You come back to a country rocked by strikes as millions of returning soldiers fought for better working conditions and salaries. How 8 years later, in 1926, the country is brought almost to a standstill with strike after strike. Imagine only ten years later, in 1929, and the economy collapses. Millions become unemployed, more lives are destroyed. In fact, unemployment more than doubles in under two years, from 1 million in 1929 to 2.5 million in 1931. And this lasts for 4 long years, until unemployment slowly recovers from 1933.

Imagine millions of people having to work their way back out of poverty. There is no proper social security or welfare till 1931, after the poor take to the streets. And remember the missing sons, fathers, brothers, husbands and fiancés.

Imagine the millions of employed women during the Great War, who have had to give their jobs back to returning men. Imagine that nearly 10% of women can no longer find a husband to support them, because those men no longer exist.

Imagine recovering from this, only to find Europe turning fascist. The Great War, only 17 years ago, is now called The War to End All War, because surely no country could survive such a devastating conflict again?

And yet, from 1936, with the Spanish Civil War, the German bombing of Spanish civilians, the German invasion of Czechoslovakia, the rise of fascism in Italy, who take war to Africa, you become aware that a new World War seems inevitable. You watch the rise of Hitler.

And what you find most difficult to understand is how it is happening again. Yes, you and millions of others suffered terribly. But astonishingly, the people who suffered most were the rich. The Prime Minister lost a son, and Bonar Law, a future Prime Minister lost two. Anthony Eden, another future Prime Minister, lost two brothers.

Yet, here are these politicians leading us back into war.

What do you do?

This is what Priestley did.

Priestley became a political voice. He wanted a better world. In his radio broadcasts during World War 2 he became the voice of the people, so 40% of the population listened to his broadcasts. That's double the figures for Bake-Off, and three times the figures for Strictly Come Dancing, the top two TV shows of 2016, 2017 and 2018. Priestley is a superstar.

Then he gave this up, forced out, denied a voice because he was too socialist. Churchill questioned the BBC, complaining about Priestley: "He's far from friendly to the government and I should not be too sure about him on larger issues."

And then the war ends. It is 1945.

How do you make your voice heard? How do you shape and reflect the mood of the nation? You write a play in which you try to show people what went wrong with society's values, what went wrong with the ruling classes, and how a new generation can make sure that these mistakes are never repeated.

You write a play which brings together all your skills as a writer, and all your political views as a socialist. The timing is perfect. Astonishingly, the mood of the nation is with you, and with the greatest landslide, the most unexpected election victory of all time happens before your eyes.

Britain gets rid of its hero Churchill, his whole government, and demands a better future for the ordinary man. A socialist revolution is born.

So, come back in time with me to study this incredibly influential play.

<u>Timeline of An Inspector Calls</u>

Other guides will give you a summary of the plot here, telling you what happens in each act. I'm not going to do that, because I am an English teacher and I want you to read the play!

But, all the plot is contained in this timeline, which is even more useful. Because timeline is crucial to understanding whether Eva is one person.

Gerald, Arthur and Sybil's attempts to dismiss their actions as unimportant, because they claim all their actions could have happened to different girls.

Yet none of the characters who describe her – Birling, Sheila, Eric, Gerald and The Inspector, say anything about her physical appearance which is contradicted by the other characters. In fact, they all believe it is the same girl because she sounds the same to them in each encounter.

This isn't just true about her "pretty" looks, but also her upbringing. Birling says he thinks she was "country bred", "lively" and "pretty". We find out her parents are dead, that she was sacked from a factory and a shop. Moreover, her personality sounds the same to each of them – willing to stand up for herself in the factory and with Eric, out of place at the Palace bar in the views of both Gerald and Eric, who both call her "a good sport".

Now we shall see that the chronology of the timeline also matches exactly:

Eva is employed at Birling's summer 1909
"she'd been working in one of our machine shops for over a year"

Eva is sacked from Birlings in the last week of September 1910
"This girl left us nearly two years ago. Let me see – it must have been in the early autumn of nineteen-ten.

Inspector: Yes. End of September, nineteen-ten."

October and November 1910. Two months of probable unemployment

Eva is employed at Milwards, beginning of December 1910
"And it happened that at the beginning of December that year – nineteen-ten – there was a good deal of influenza about and Milwards suddenly found themselves short handed."

January to February 1911, works at Milwards
"After about a couple of months, just when she felt she was settling down nicely, they told her she'd have to go."

Eva is sacked by Milwards at the end of February 1911

March 1911, Eva is probably unemployed, or possibly meets Gerald

March/April to September 1911, Eva is Gerald's mistress
"Were you seeing her last spring and summer, during that time you hardly came near me?"

Gerald rejects Eva, the first week in September 1911
<u>Gerald</u>: I can tell you exactly. In the first week of September".

September, October and possibly some of November 1911, Eva lives off her savings at a seaside.
"<u>Inspector</u>: Yes. She went away for about two months. To some seaside place."

November 1911, Eva meets Eric at the Palace bar.
"<u>Inspector</u>: (*To* Eric.) When did you first meet this girl?

<u>Eric</u>: One night last November."

November 1911, Eva probably survives through prostitution, going back to the Palace bar for two weeks.
"<u>Inspector</u>: When did you meet her again?

<u>Eric</u>: About a fortnight afterwards."

Late November or December 1911, Eva begins a relationship with Eric
"<u>Inspector</u>: (*To* Eric.) did you arrange to see each other after that?

<u>Eric</u>: Yes."

December 1911, Eva falls pregnant
"<u>Eric</u>: Yes. And the next time – or the time after that – she told me she thought she was going to have a baby."

December 1911 to February or March 1912, Eva gets money from Eric.
<u>Eric</u>: I suppose – about fifty pounds all told."

February or March 1912, Eva breaks off the relationship or arrangement with Eric
"<u>Inspector</u>: The girl discovered that this money you were giving her was stolen, didn't she?

<u>Eric</u>: (*miserably*) Yes. That was the worst of all. She wouldn't take any more, and she didn't want to see me again."

End of March 1912, Eva seeks help from Mrs Birling's charity, "The Brumley Women's Charity Organisation". It is refused.
"<u>Inspector</u>: there was a meeting of the interviewing committee two weeks ago?

First week in April 1912, Eva commits suicide.
"It is an evening in spring, 1912."

"Birling: The Titanic – she sails next week".
(The Titanic set sail on 10th of April, and sunk on April 14th)

J B Priestley, Biography and Context

(The bold sections show you how to use this context when writing about the play. That's the only reason to write about context.)

Priestley was born in Bradford in Yorkshire 1894.
When he writes about Brumley, he is fictionalising a town and people he knows well.

His father was a school teacher.
We can see this reflected in the didactic tone of the play, and how The Inspector works, trying to teach the Birlings a lesson. Priestley is also trying to teach his audience the same lesson.

He wanted to become a writer, but decided not to go to university, thinking he would learn more about the world by experience.
We can perhaps see this reflected in his portrayal of Eric, who went to Oxford or Cambridge, and appears to have learned nothing until The Inspector arrives to teach him about social responsibility.

So, he became a junior clerk at a wool firm when he was 16, in 1910.
This is a similarity with Eva, who also works in textiles. She has probably, like Priestley, begun work there in 1910, because she is tipped for promotion in 1911.

His first piece of writing was published on 14th of December 1912, when he was 18.
1912 is a key turning point in Priestley's life, and is therefore a possible reason he fixes on this year as the key turning point in Eva's life.

It is also when Eva herself becomes a writer, writing in the diary which The Inspector uncovers. It is easy to forget this!

He joined the army in 1914, aged 20, not as an officer.
This choice shows how he would see himself as different to the sons of the wealthy, like Eric and Gerald, who would have joined up or been conscripted as officers.

He was seriously injured in June 1916, came home to convalesce and then trained as an officer. He returned in 1917, but was then gassed, and returned home to work in administrative jobs in the army.
When the Inspector warns the Birlings about learning their lesson in 'fire and blood and anguish', he is talking from bitter experience of the slaughter in the war.

It is probably the war which convinced him to be a socialist.
He wrote autobiographically in Margin Released (1962) of the stupidity of its upper-class generals:

"The British command specialised in throwing men away for nothing … killed most of my friends as surely as if those cavalry generals had come out of the chateaux with polo mallets and beaten their brains out. Call this class prejudice if you like, so long as you remember … that I went into that war without any such prejudice, free of any class feeling. No doubt I came out of it with a chip on my shoulder; a big, heavy chip, probably some friend's thigh-bone."

The officer class would have been made up of men like Gerald and Eric and Birling. The way they treat Eva, as a simple casualty of capitalism is exactly the way he accuses the generals of throwing away the lives of their men, the "John Smiths".

During the war, he wrote poetry and published an anthology privately. However, when he returned he destroyed most copies.

Many students assume that writers just write stuff down. In fact, they agonise over every word. As you see here, there was so much to correct in the poems, that he simply destroyed them. Remember this when we analyse particular words and phrases – yes, Priestley really did mean to use exactly those words, and it really is worth asking exactly why he chose them.

After the war, he went to Cambridge. He completed his degree in two years instead of three.

Arguably this is where he would have met men exactly like Eric and Gerald for the first time. Being older, and having survived the war, he is clearly in a real hurry to make progress in life. We can perhaps see this reflected when The Inspector says, "we haven't much time" and in the way Priestley makes Sheila repeat this.

He married his childhood sweetheart from Bradford, where he lived. He went to London to work as a writer.

He wrote as a freelance writer: reviews, fiction, non-fiction, biography, anything to get published. He worked for a publisher as a reader, and also had four novels published, his fourth being most successful, <u>The Good Companions</u>, in 1929. This novel is a largely comic portrait of people – while it features the working classes, it taps in to the mood of escapism in the 1920s.

He published 50 more plays in his lifetime.

We can argue that the attraction of the plays is the ability to engage directly with the public and use social commentary. His writing became much more politically active during The Depression in the 1930s.

His publisher, Victor Gollancz, asked him to tour the country to see the effects of The Depression in 1933, and the result of this was published as <u>English Journey</u>, a massive success.

Priestley has a special interest in social reform based on what he has seen of the lives of the working classes and the unemployed. He dramatises this through Eva, and also teaches his audience by explicitly relating her to "the millions of Eva Smiths, and the millions of John Smiths" in the country.

He became a prolific writer with numerous plays and pieces of autobiography. He also went to America frequently and worked as a script writer.

He became a broadcaster in 1939. He had a very successful radio show during World War 2 which was broadcast as 'Postscripts' which came on just after the news. Although often critical of the government, they were designed to be uplifting for morale.

He was seen by many as the voice of the people after his famous broadcast on Dunkirk:

"But now - look - this little steamer, like all her brave and battered sisters, is immortal. She'll go sailing proudly down the years in the epic of Dunkirk. And our great grand-children, when they learn how we began this War by snatching glory out of defeat, and then swept on to victory, may also learn how the little holiday steamers made an excursion to hell and came back glorious."

You can listen to it here (https://www.youtube.com/watch?v=EYNv4ozHJDw)

We can see here that he is keen to celebrate the ordinary man and woman, and how they can put an end to "hell". This is the same message as his play: vote for socialism, not just for a more just society, but to put an end to war.

He continued to write novels and plays during the war.
Priestley made moral choices, choosing to be good, rather than employed, or secure financially. These personal choices, which his audience in 1945 would remember, give him credibility, an imprimatur of morality. (Look it up, it's a really useful word).

In the 1930s, during the Great Depression, Priestley became very concerned about the inequalities in Britain, and the huge rise in unemployment. He even helped set up a new political party, the Common Wealth Party in 1942. It merged with the Labour Party in 1945. He stood for parliament as an independent MP in 1945, but was not elected. He was never a member of the Labour Party.

We can see from this how the war increased the public appetite for a more equal society. People could see how unequal society was before the war, and they contrasted this with how massive employment was possible during the war. They noticed millions more jobs for women. People started to ask what kind of future was worth dying for. Priestley deliberately wrote a socialist play to answer that question. He thought a society that cared for everyone else in it, where the rich made sure they didn't exploit the poor was worth fighting for. He wrote the play to change society.

He first performed An Inspector Calls in Russia as there were no theatres available in London.

He still wrote campaigning literature after the war, feeling that a lot of the promise of the 1945 election had not come to fruition in the 1950s.

One piece, 'Britain and the Nuclear Bombs' was so critical at the British development of nuclear weapons that it led to a huge response from readers of the New Statesman. This led to the setting up of CND, the campaign for nuclear disarmament, and Priestley became its vice president.

He was active in the early movement toward a United Nations because he thought it was so important to prevent further wars. He was a delegate to UNESCO, where he met his third wife.

We can see in this that he lived out the moral lessons of The Inspector, wanted a society based on people looking after each other, and believing that the greatest threat was future war. When we deal with the ending of the play you will see how it is an attack on war, just as much as an attack on the Birlings' exploitation of the working classes.

He turned down a knighthood and a peerage, as both would be awarded by political parties. However, he did accept the Order of Merit in 1977, as this is a gift made entirely by the Queen, without political overtones.

This allows us to see how critical he would like us to be about the titles in the play: Sir Croft, Gerald's father is so much of a snob he doesn't even celebrate Gerald's engagement to Sheila, who comes from a family he sees as socially inferior. Birling's craving for a "knighthood", not having served his community in any way, reveals why we should dislike him.

He died in 1984 having published over 150 books.

The Detective Story: Whodunit?

The play can be read as a detective story in which we try to work out the guilty party. Priestley plays with the conventions. Instead of waiting till the end to find out who the guilty party is, he shows us that they are all guilty.

"A **whodunit** or **whodunnit** (for "Who [has] done it?" or "Who did it?") is a complex, plot-driven variety of the detective story in which the audience is given the opportunity to engage in the same process of deduction as the protagonist throughout the investigation of a crime. The reader or viewer is provided with the clues from which the identity of the perpetrator may be deduced before the story provides the revelation itself at its climax. The investigation is usually conducted by an eccentric, amateur, or semi-professional detective." (Wikipedia)

Some readers see the play as an exercise in deciding who is most guilty. This is an interesting question which you will have think about when reading about each character.

How Does Priestley Use the Whodunit Genre to Make us Think Like Detectives?

How does the audience engage in deduction? What are the clues? What are the plot twists?

1. Gerald being away in the summer: "except for all last summer, when you never came near me, and I wondered what had happened to you."
2. Eric laughing about this: *"Eric suddenly guffaws"*.
3. Eric interrupting himself when he remembers Eva: "<u>Eric</u>: (*eagerly*) Yes, I remember – (*but he checks himself*.)"
4. The effect Sheila notices about The Inspector: "<u>Sheila</u>: (*slowly*) It's queer – very queer - (she *looks at them reflectively*.)"
5. The Inspectors words about affecting the young ones: "(*coolly*) we often do on the young ones. They're more impressionable."
6. Sheila working out that Eric is the father of Eva's child before her mother does: "(*distressed*) Now, mother – don't you see?"
7. Gerald finding out he is not a real inspector: "There isn't any such inspector. We've been had."
8. Whether it is all the same girl, or different photographs of different girls: "He could have used a different photograph each time and we'd be none the wiser."
9. The phone call to the infirmary saying that there is no dead girl: "No girl has died in there today."
10. The name of Inspector Goole: "can you tell me if an Inspector Goole has joined your staff lately . . . Goole."
11. The second phone call – how did they kill the new girl: "That was the police. A girl has just died."
12. Who is the new inspector? Will it also be Goole?: "And a police inspector is on his way here – to ask some – questions…"

For the first two acts, we can be confident that we are in the plot of a mystery like Murder on the Orient Express, by Agatha Christie in 1934. (Spoiler alert – in Christie's novel we find out at the end that there is no single murderer – they are all guilty of participating in the same murder). The similarity is deliberate.

However, Priestley plays with the genre of the Whodunit in Act 3. At first, we wonder how The Inspector is the guilty party, how did he carry out an elaborate hoax?

Is the Inspector the Killer?

Many students decide that The Inspector is a murderer. That he somehow keeps the real Eva locked up. He then waits for the Birlings to argue about how they were responsible for her death, or not responsible, and then, to teach them a lesson, he kills her.

I'm sorry to say this is rubbish:
1. He could teach exactly the same lesson if he had killed her at the start.
2. If the Inspector is a murderer, the lesson that he teaches, "we are all of one body", becomes ridiculous. You can't look after each other by killing each other. Killing Eva would teach the opposite of his lesson.
3. The only way he could find out if they had learned his lesson, and all accepted responsibility, is to listen to the conversation live, as we do. He would not be able to then kill Eva somewhere else at the same time.
4. Priestley couldn't introduce the supernatural element of 'Goole' if he simply expected the audience to decide The Inspector was a real person, who was also a murderer.

Is God a Killer?
The only way you can back the theory that The Inspector kills Eva on purpose is to see him as, not just supernatural, but God. In this reading, The Inspector sacrifices Eva in order to correct the sins of the ruling classes. This is what God does in sacrificing Jesus, who dies to save mankind from sin. It is also a way of teaching mankind about social responsibility, just as The Inspector does. Although there is evidence that Priestley believed in the idea of a soul, there is also evidence that he did not like the power of the church.

If we follow this interpretation, God resurrects Jesus. Here, The Inspector can't resurrect her, only the Birlings can do that.

So, if you want to view The Inspector as caring and compassionate, while at the same time a ruthless murderer, you can. But only if you point out that he is trying to say that is exactly how God behaves, even in the New Testament.

If you do argue that, you can't argue that this is his main message in the play. It has to be a hidden or coded message. Why? Because the majority of his audience was Christian. He simply couldn't afford to alienate them, as they wouldn't then listen to his socialist message. And the socialist message is his main reason for writing the play.

Then there is the more profound mystery of the second death. Because this happens right at the final curtain, Priestley asks us to go back over the events of the play, as detectives ourselves, to work out how the death occurred.

This should make Priestley's teaching, his socialist message, much more relatable to his audience – they are well versed in this genre of fiction, and would be both familiar with his techniques, and surprised at how he has subverted the whodunit genre with the final twist.

The Morality Play

The Morality Play was popular in the 15th and 16th centuries, just before Shakespeare's time. They were allegorical plays, in which the plots taught a moral lesson. The characters all represented moral qualities. They would either be a virtue (such as *honesty*, or *charity*), or a vice (such as *lust* or *greed*).

The characters might also represent wider types or ideas, for example *youth*, or *age*.

"Together with the mystery play and the miracle play, the morality play is one of the three main types of vernacular drama produced during the Middle Ages. The action of the morality play centres on a hero, such as Mankind, whose inherent weaknesses are assaulted by such personified diabolic forces as the Seven Deadly Sins but who may choose redemption and enlist the aid of such figures as the Four Daughters of God (Mercy, Justice, Temperance, and Truth)." (Britannica.com)

We can clearly see how Priestley is playing with these ideas. His play certainly teaches a moral lesson, characters certainly represent wider types: the upper classes, the working classes, the older and younger generations, gender roles for men and women.

The characters are given the choice of redemption – to admit what they have done wrong. Regardless of whether The Inspector was real, and regardless of whether it was all to the same girl – the nature of their wrongdoing, their sin, is still exactly the same.

7 Deadly Sins List & Meanings

1. **Envy** = the desire to have an item or experience that someone else possesses
2. **Gluttony** = excessive ongoing consumption of food or drink
3. **Greed** or **Avarice** = an excessive pursuit of material possessions
4. **Lust** = an uncontrollable passion or longing, especially for sexual desires
5. **Pride** = excessive view of one's self without regard to others.
6. **Sloth** = excessive laziness or the failure to act and utilize one's talents
7. **Wrath** = uncontrollable feelings of anger and hate towards another person

We can easily attach some of these to the characters:

- Arthur Birling clearly personifies Greed or Avarice.
- Sheila clearly personifies Envy
- Gerald personifies Lust (and capitalist Greed)
- Eric personifies Gluttony (and this causes Lust through his alcohol abuse)
- Sybil Birling clearly personifies Pride

Looked at in these simple terms, Priestley might also be suggesting that the characters who represent the most deadly sins, having more than one, are therefore the most guilty. Looked at this way he is most concerned about the sexual exploitation of women, represented by Gerald's and Eric's exploitation of Eva.

If you are writing an essay on who is most guilty, this will be a winning argument!

Morality plays are also strongly rooted in the Christian tradition – it is Christian moral values which they taught. Priestley also uses Christian language, deliberately using the words of the Anglican service.

So, when The Inspector teaches his final lesson, that "we are all members of one body", Priestley is deliberately making a biblical reference – to Romans and Corinthians, which are 'books' in The Bible.

Romans 12:5
"So we, being many, are one body in Christ, and every one members one of another."

1 Corinthians 10:17
"For we being many are one bread, and one body: for we are all partakers of that one bread."

(King James Version of The Bible)

His audience might not know The Bible well enough to quote these two references. However, they would all be familiar with the words of the communion:

"**Breaking of the Bread**
The president breaks the consecrated bread.

We break this bread
to share in the body of Christ.

All
Though we are many, we are one body,
because we all share in one bread."

Because the majority of his audience (about 80%) were still practising Christians at the end of the war, Priestley is keen to link his socialist message to a Christian message.

If his audience are already Christian, it is a smaller step to embracing the same message if socialism uses the same words as the church and The Bible.

You can clearly argue that Priestley deliberately uses the language of the Anglican communion to connect with his Christian audience. And you should argue that he wants to show how a truly Christian society would also have to be a socialist society.

Opening Stage Directions

The opening stage directions are very detailed, at 415 words long. We could almost say that they appear obsessive.

These stage directions reveal Priestley's didactic intentions: he wants to teach us through the entertainment of the play. Everything on stage represents something to Priestley, which is why he is so particular. His message depends on the actors understanding the significance of each part of the set, and of how they should relate to each other.

Contrast this with Shakespeare, where stage directions only appear to mark exits and entrances. Any clue as to relevant props, such as "torches" to signify night, are only found in the dialogue. Similarly, action is also revealed through dialogue:
"I bite my thumb at you…"
"It is her custom to stand thus…"
"Be not amazed…"
"Look how our partner stands rapt withal…" etc.

What You Should Learn About the Stage Directions

The Three Unities
Priestley is following the Greek tradition in sticking to the three unities. The Greeks invented theatre, and invented the idea of Tragedy. The unities come:

"from Aristotle's Poetics, holding that a play should have one unified plot (unity of action) and that all the action should occur within one day (unity of time) and be limited to a single locale (unity of place)" (collinsdictionary.com)

Priestley wants his audience to know they are watching a play which he has crafted. (Did you know a 'wright' is a craftsman, a maker? This is why we have the word **playwright**, not playwrite).

Aristotle wrote about his unities as necessary parts of a tragedy. Priestley is consequently telling us that the story which unfolds is therefore a tragedy. This is highly unusual, because in this tragedy there is only one death – and even that is uncertain, at the end.

However, in this way he shows us that the events are symbolic – Eva's death, and second death, represent the tragedies of the First and Second World Wars, as you will learn later.

The other tragedy is the fate of the working classes, who have been exploited by the ruling classes. Eva is not just a character, she is a symbol of the millions of Eva Smiths and John Smiths: they are victimised as she is.

The Date

Priestley chooses "an evening in Spring, 1912" because it is just before The First World War. It is also essential to him because it places the play during the context of women's campaign for the vote (suffrage), and the Suffragettes.

1912 is also crucial in that he can begin the play with a tragedy, the sinking of the Titanic in April of 1912. We know that it is just about to happen, when Birling talks about it being "unsinkable". Priestley isn't just trying to discredit Birling for his stupidity: the dramatic irony of us knowing the Titanic will sink also invites us to think of the play as a tragedy.

We can also infer that "Spring" is symbolic of rebirth, optimism, and hope. Perhaps he suggests at the beginning of the play that hope is still possible. This is very relevant to his message – the audience can learn from the play and vote for a socialist future, in which men don't just "look after their own family" but remember their social responsibility: "we are all responsible for each other".

Symbolic Setting v Realistic Setting
Priestley does not care "if a realistic set is used", but is very careful to demand what impression needs to be created for his symbolism to work.

The furniture has to reveal that this is a dysfunctional family. It is "heavily comfortable", which is almost a contradiction, an oxymoron. He then contrasts this with "not cosy and homelike". We understand that, despite their wealth and luxury, the Birlings are not at home with each other.

Remember, though, that this also represents all the upper classes.

Priestley's tone suggests that he prefers a setting which is symbolic. One clue to this is that he lists the requirements of the realistic set first, as people do when they wish to then offer a winning counter argument – in this case, the symbolic setting last.

He also lists the difficulties of a realistic set, involving lots of furniture moving, as a way to dissuade the producer from having a realistic set. So, he promotes a symbolic setting:

"Producers who wish to avoid this tricky business, which involves two re-settings of the scene and some very accurate adjustments of the extra flats necessary would be well advised to dispense with an ordinary realistic set if only because the dining-table becomes a nuisance."

Look at how he juxtaposes "realistic" with "ordinary", suggesting that a much better theatrical effect involves dispensing with realism. Be realistic if you want to be boring, but symbolic if you want to be interesting, he seems to be saying.

There are real physical details. But they all have symbolic meanings. Let's see how:

1. *"EDNA is just clearing the table"*.

It is important that we see the contrast between Edna, the symbol of the working classes, being made to work while the privileged Birlings celebrate idly.

2. **The table** *"has no cloth".*
   Why specify this detail? Perhaps it suggests that the Birlings don't quite understand proper etiquette. Not only should there be a cloth, but it should also be white.

   This may suggest that they incorrectly see themselves as having higher status – this will be the reason that Sybil has for turning her charity away from Eva, dismissing her as "girls of that class".

   Perhaps Priestley is suggesting that the white table cloth is just a veneer, just like the respectability of the upper classes. As the Inspector says, he can't always "tell the difference" between "respectable" and "criminal" when he meets the ruling classes.

   Or, perhaps white is too symbolic of goodness and innocence, which does not fit with his view of the Birlings, who are all guilty.

   Which interpretation do you prefer?

3. **Etiquette**
   Priestley specifies that there must be *"champagne glasses,"* cleared away, *"then replacing them with decanter of port"* and insists *"Port glasses are already on the table."* This does precisely follow Edwardian etiquette. However, it also strongly emphasises the amount of alcohol being consumed. Partly this will be to make it easier to show how much Eric is drinking.

   More than this, because it was etiquette, all the upper classes were expected to entertain guests and drink this way. It emphasises how much the ruling classes actually drank, so that we can criticise them for their habit.

   It also questions their judgment. How much of Eva's tragedy is caused by drunkenness? We'll think about this with Gerald and Eric's dealings with Eva.

   A final implication might be that all upper-class families rely on this ritual at dinner to cover up their lack of family feeling. They simply need the alcohol to get through the meal because they don't necessarily enjoy each other's company.

4. *"All five are in evening dress of the period, the men in tails and white ties, not dinner-jackets."*
   This again emphasises how difficult it must be for them to relax. Dinner jackets are far more comfortable, but Priestley forbids this.

This will force the male characters to appear a bit stiff and, because they won't want to sit on their "tails", they will have to adjust them every time they move.

This will look both uncomfortable and a bit like a ritual. In this way Priestley could be showing how class divisions are actually unnatural, and also damage the upper classes. You will see this when we look at the role of women, and when you read about the fate of upper-class sons in The First World War.

Lighting
His instructions for the lighting also show how keen he is for everything to be symbolic:

> *"The lighting should be pink and intimate until The Inspector arrives and then it should be brighter and harder".*

Notice that the pink lighting is "intimate" which contradicts the impression of the furniture which was "not cosy". This is a subtle way of indicating that the family is not harmonious. It is an attempt at intimacy, but it can't work because they are all so busy deceiving themselves or each other.

The idea of deceit is suggested by the word "pink", which we associate with the phrase 'rose tinted spectacles', indicating a desire to choose to see yourself or circumstances in a false light – a positive one.

This is why The Inspector's arrival is timed with a "brighter" and "harder" light. Not only does this suggest the lighting should be whiter, but it also gives the symbolic reason – The Inspector is going to reveal the hard truth; he is going to make the family see things as they really are, rather than through the rose tinted "pink" light.

Later in the play Sheila will notice that the timing of The Inspector's arrival is important – "Sheila: (sharply attentive) Is that when The Inspector came, just after father had said that?". The change in lighting will make it much easier for the audience to remember this moment clearly.

More than that, though, it will suggest that The Inspector has greater, or supernatural, powers. He somehow appears because of Birling's words, almost as though he is summoned by them, like an incantation to invoke a spirit. This is emphasised by his effect on the lighting, the life of the stage, again implying a supernatural power.

Priestley will link this to his choice of name for The Inspector, "Goole", which is a homophone for 'ghoul' or ghost.

Time and The Future
Calling the Inspector "Goole" taps into his audience's collective knowledge of <u>A Christmas Carol,</u> by Charles Dickens. Writers often use deliberate allusions like this to remind the audience of texts they already know. You have already seen this with the communion service, <u>Murder on the Orient Express,</u> and <u>The Bible</u>. No, these allusions

are not coincidences, they are ways of telling his audience that his ideas are relevant – they are connected to ideas his audience already know.

A Christmas Carol

This is another didactic text or, if you like, a morality tale. Here the job of the ghosts is to teach the protagonist, Scrooge, the consequences of his behaviour. They are named after time: the ghosts of Christmas past, present and future.

Just like Inspector Goole, their job is to teach a character about the effect that actions in the past have on the present and the future. They also teach that the future can be changed by making a moral change, and choosing to look after your fellow man. In this case, Scrooge has to change his behaviour to all men, but specifically, to Bob Cratchit, his employee. So, we could argue that Inspector Goole is most like Dickens' "Ghost of Christmas Yet to Come".

His audience would clearly see the parallel between this and the Birlings' exploitation of Eva.

Priestley emphasises this by using the same dramatic device as Dickens. Scrooge is given a glimpse of a tragic future for Bob and his family, just as the Birlings are given a tragic future for Eva and her baby. Unlike Scrooge, they ignore the warning, and it appears that this causes Eva to die at the ending of the play.

Why Doesn't Priestley Just Tell Us!?

If Priestley is going to write out such long stage directions, why doesn't he just tell the director, 'it is important that the audience realise that The Inspector is a ghost from the future". After all, Dickens tells his reader this very clearly, calling him "The Ghost of Christmas Yet to Come".

Some possible reasons:

In this guide I'll show you how Gerald, Eric and Sheila can be viewed in two ways, as morally much worse than they appear.

This ambiguity seems to be important to Priestley. Yes, he wants to entertain us. But he also wants his audience to keep thinking about these characters and their motives, because that will then make the audience question their own motives and actions. It is therefore essential for him to introduce ambiguities for each character – if they are simply black and white, good or bad, we wouldn't need to think about them once the play is over.

This is how he is trying to influence the future – he wants to change how his audience make moral choices, and political choices, later on.

I would argue that this is the main point of all the puzzles in the play – to keep the audience thinking days, weeks and years after they have experienced the play, as you will see later in the guide.

How Ambiguity is used to Introduce the Characters

The Birlings are separated:

"the four Birling's and Gerald are seated at the table, with Arthur Birling at one end, his wife at the other".

This was not customary in Edwardian times. Although the host and his wife could choose to sit separately, they often sat opposite each other at the centre.

- Priestley instead chooses to symbolise a great distance between Arthur Birling and Sybil Birling.

- Possibly he feels that one is much guiltier in their treatment toward Eva – you will decide later.

- Possibly he wants to show that they are linked only by rank and position in society, and not by love.

- Possibly he wants to show that they are surrounding their children, either protectively, or as an attack, literally on their flanks.

Again, you will have to decide.

A contemporary audience would instinctively be on the lookout for signs of conflict between them, and between the parents in one camp, and Eric and Sheila on the other. This separation is obvious to a modern audience seeing the play, but even more obvious to Priestley's in 1945.

Power Relationships
Priestley also wants the director and actor to think very carefully about the power relationships in the play. Which end is the head of the table? Normally this is quite clear in etiquette – the male host sits at the end. His wife does not. This emphasises quite clearly where status and power truly lie in a patriarchal society.

Priestley deliberately breaks this tradition by having two heads – Birling at one end, Mrs Birling at the other. He might be suggesting that Sybil sees herself as superior to her husband.

Or, he might be signalling that this moment, in 1912, symbolises the rise of female power, as it coincides with the birth of the Suffragettes. We shall see that in 1945, women were uppermost in Priestley's mind, especially because they could all now vote, but in 1912, no woman could.

Why Eric is the odd one out
This seating plan is also obviously an odd number, and the odd one out will be Eric. This only works, however, if Sybil and her husband are at opposite ends – if she moves to the

middle, there are four in the middle, and Birling is in his proper place at the head of the table. If Priestley staged it that way, we would not question his authority so quickly.

Eric becomes increasingly important in Act 1, and Priestley wants to make this inevitable *"Eric downstage and Sheila and Gerald seated upstage."* "Downstage" means that Eric is closer to the audience than Sheila and Gerald, even though they are at the centre of most of the conversation at the start.

This is because Priestley wants us to decide what Eric has to hide. The director is allowed to choose whether we notice his drinking, and whether he is drunk. However, once he begins to interrupt, Priestley is determined we must notice this, so he sits him at the front. In this way he is already preparing us for the twist at the end of Act 2 where we find out that Eric is a drunk and Eric is the father of Eva's child.

Stage Directions about the Characters

A Character is a Construct

Ok, the most important thing to remember is that characters are never real people. They are made or constructed. Examiners refer to them as "a construct", and students who understand this get the top grades.

But, English Professors and authors also see characters as "a construct". This means that every character is created for a reason, indeed for lots of reasons. All of those reasons will involve influencing the reader or audience.

When you start asking, "How is the author trying to influence me?" you are becoming a proper student of literature. You get even better when you ask, "How is the author trying to influence people of the time?" as well.

Arthur Birling

What's wrong with Birling?

Priestley wants us to question Birling's authority, because he represents capitalism, not just wealth. For example, Gerald's family are in the same business, textile factory owners. However, his wealth is inherited – his father knighted "Sir George Croft" and his mother "Lady Croft". Priestley wants to criticise his level of society, which he does through Gerald.

But Priestley sees the capitalists, the "hard headed man of business", as much more of a social problem than the aristocracy, because there are more of them in 1945, and they affect more working-class people through their low wages and working conditions.

Priestley questions capitalism itself when he questions Birling's authority. Structurally, it is why he chooses to start the play with Birling. He is showing that capitalism is the root cause, the start, of Eva's problem.

But, we shall see that capitalism is not the main cause. This is because Priestley believes that capitalism can be made to work in moral ways, so that people still help each other. Perhaps this is why he never joined the Labour Party. He does not want to destroy capitalism: he wants to make it work for a much fairer society.

How Priestley Constructs Birling

Remember, each character is not a real person. They are a construct. They are made. Examiners love you to use the phrase 'a construct', as in 'Birling is a construct who represents the dangers of capitalism'.

Birling *"is…heavy-looking"*. This helps us see Birling as a construct:

1. It will work symbolically with his personification of 'Greed' as one of the Seven Deadly Sins. This will also signify all business men, and the capitalist system are greedy.

2. It will provide a contrast with The Inspector, who will have a "massive" appearance, not in size, but in impact, suggesting that the working classes can match the power of the ruling classes.
3. It can suggest that he is indulgent, self-satisfied, and slow. Slowing Birling down is actually the most likely way an actor could convey heaviness, and we would not just associate this with bad health, but also with stupidity. Priestley will emphasise this with Birling's predictions, whose dramatic irony will reveal him as utterly wrong.

He is also a *"rather portentous",* which suggests he is full of self-importance and trying to impress. We are therefore already critical of him at first sight, and also feel superior to him. This is another way that Priestley questions the authority of the rich.

He has *"fairly easy manners"*, implying how happy and perhaps confident he is of getting the knighthood he so craves, and how confident he is that Gerald will marry Sheila.

Priestley describes him as *"but rather provincial in this speech."* Perhaps this suggests that he should not be so pleased with himself, he is nouveau riche*, and therefore looked down upon by those born into the upper classes. (*This was a phrase used to describe the wealthy who had earned their wealth. The implication was that this sort of wealth was nowhere near as desirable as that acquired through family inheritance, through breeding, through being part of the nobility, perhaps like Gerald.)

Alternatively, it can also help with The Inspector's message that we are all the same, "members of one body", and therefore class distinctions are an illusion. It might teach that class distinctions are a damaging social construct which only have power because we choose to believe in them.

Finally, Priestley also wants to contrast this with Birling's wife.

Sybil Birling

"His wife is about fifty". Priestley insists that Birling should be slightly older, "in his middle fifties". This pattern will be deliberately echoed in the relative ages of their daughter Sheila and her older fiancé Gerald. This implies that the Birlings were once just like Sheila and Gerald, which will be important when we ask ourselves at the end of the play if they have truly learned The Inspector's lesson. (If they share the same age gap as Arthur and Sybil, perhaps they are more likely to marry, and perhaps Sheila is therefore less likely to live out the lesson The Inspector teaches her).

What's wrong with Sibyl Birling?
Sybil is *"a rather cold woman and her husband's social superior".* This juxtaposition suggests that Priestley believes being socially "superior" also makes a person "cold" and unfeeling towards others. He wants to change this in his audience.

Another reason for this is to emphasise the division between husband and wife, so that there is an element of conflict which matches the seating arrangement.

Another ambiguity is also deliberately placed in front of us. Did she marry Arthur because she loved him, therefore ignoring his lower social status? This is a parallel with Gerald choosing to marry Sheila, who has a lower social status and is "not good enough" for Gerald in the eyes of his parents. After the end of the play, we ask if this parallel will continue, and if Sheila will therefore marry Gerald.

Sheila Birling

What is wrong with Sheila?
"a pretty girl in her early twenties, very pleased with life and rather excited."
We can see that at the start of the play Priestley wants us to see Sheila as a "girl", rather than a woman. This is surprising to a modern audience, especially as "early twenties" implies an age of around 23.

He also seems to be a bit dismissive of her: telling us she is "excited" would tell us that she is excited by the moment – she is going to be engaged tonight, and knows this because that is what the dinner is for. However, the modifier, "rather" also implies criticism, as though Priestley is suggesting she is too "excited", and not in proper control of her emotions.

Sheila is a construct
He also links this directly to her class. It is her wealth and status which mean that she is "very pleased with life". This interestingly echoes the description of Birling, as "portentous", being very pleased with himself. At least at the start of the play she is very much like her father who, we will see, is also excited about a probable Knighthood.

When we get to the end of the play you will have to decide if she has crossed a threshold into womanhood, or whether she is still a "girl", who will still follow her father's wishes, and marry Gerald, partly for his status.

Gerald Croft

What's wrong with Gerald?
"Gerald croft is an attractive chap about thirty, rather too manly to be a dandy but very much the well-bred young man-about-town."

Gerald is described as "an attractive chap". This is the same dismissive language he uses to describe Sheila. Instead of being called a man, he is a "chap". Perhaps Priestley is suggesting that the upper classes are too privileged to face real life, and without the challenge of making their way in their world, they can never be considered true men.

Alternatively, it may be looking at Gerald's self-obsession and self-interest, and suggesting that his inherited wealth prevents him from truly growing up. He never becomes a real man in Priestley's eyes because he doesn't accept responsibility for his actions.

Gerald is a contradiction

Priestley also suggests he is vain, "rather too manly to be a dandy". The flamboyance of the word "dandy" suggests a man obsessed with his appearance. Whereas the "dandy" is obsessed with his clothes, Gerald is much more obsessed with work and sex.

This expression also suggests that Priestley doesn't just want us to dismiss Gerald. "Manly" suggests we should also find things to admire in him. You may find this a bit of a problem – how can Priestley want us to admire a man who we discover straight away has been cheating on Sheila, who he loves and wants to marry? The answer, perhaps strangely, is that Priestley simply saw this is a "manly" way to behave. Priestley had a number of affairs, and even fathered a daughter with a friend's wife:

"Priestley had a number of affairs and in later life he admitted he "enjoyed the physical relations with the sexes ... without the feelings of guilt which seems to disturb some of my distinguished colleagues" (http://spartacus-educational.com/JPriestley.htm)

But, Priestley might also be troubled by his lack of guilt. He might describe Gerald as "too manly", because he is working too hard perhaps to be attractive to women.

Certainly it is his vanity that Sheila will pick up on when she reacts to his affair with Eva as Daisy Renton. She accuses him of desiring to be flattered by Daisy's worshipping of him. "You were the wonderful fairy prince. You must have adored it, Gerald."

He has the ability to act correctly in all sorts of circumstances, as Sybil observes when he presents Sheila with her engagement ring, so that he is "very much the well-bred man about town". Being well bred does not just refer to his behaviour, but also to what Priestley's audience would call his breeding – the assumption that the upper classes were literally more refined.

Gerald represents the upper classes who inherit their wealth

Because they only married from within their own class, they become ever more perfect with each generation. This is what the word 'breeding' would have meant in 1945. It is literally genetic engineering, without science intervening – social selection did it.

Priestley, as you will have gathered by now, wants to attack this view of the upper classes. Again, he does this with his familiar technique of juxtaposition. Gerald is the "well-bred man about town", which implies that he frequents fashionable places: theatres, art galleries, restaurants, or social events.

Gerald represents sexual exploitation

But, because the setting is "in Brumley, an industrial city in the north Midlands", we question this cosmopolitan interpretation of "man about town". This isn't London. Instead of Shaftsbury Avenue, Gerald will frequent the Palace theatre, and indeed appears to go there mainly for the bar and the women he will meet there. And these women are mainly prostitutes. This "man about town" is searching for sex, rather than culture.

Priestley is already suggesting that Gerald is likely to be promiscuous (what today you would call – but not in your essays! – a bit of player).

Remember that Gerald does not just represent himself, he is a construct. He represents the other side of capitalism, those who have inherited their wealth for generations and therefore feel entitled from birth.

Priestley suggests that all those with titles, the aristocracy, living on inherited wealth, are like this – self-obsessed and immoral.

Perhaps Priestley wants us to dislike and admire Gerald at the same time. This would throw a light on how society admires those with high social status, even though we know they have done nothing to achieve that status, or to merit it. This is why Birling is so excited to get a Knighthood. It means he has arrived in society. His huge wealth alone can't do that.

Eric

What's wrong with Eric?
"Eric is in his early twenties" just like Sheila. Priestley makes them the same age, perhaps so that he can contrast the difference between them in how they have treated Eva. One argument I will put forward later is that Priestley believes Eric's treatment of Eva is far worse than Sheila's.

Another possibility is that Priestley wants his audience to consider that they are both equally damaged by their upper-class upbringing. Sheila was too "excitable", and Eric is unbalanced by having two contradictory halves. He is *"not quite at ease, half shy, half assertive"*.

He is not described as a "chap", boy, or a man, where Gerald was both a "chap" and a man, and Sheila was labelled a "girl". This is curious. One possibility is that Priestley wants us to decide for ourselves about Eric – a "man" will have learned his lessons, but a boy will not.

Because of his alcohol abuse, Eric is possibly the hardest character to judge. It may be that Priestley wants us to think hardest about him. Remember, that's why he insists that Eric must be seated "upstage".

You need to understand Capitalism and Socialism

Definition of Capitalism

"an economic system in which investment in and ownership of the means of production, distribution, and exchange of wealth is made and maintained chiefly by private individuals or corporations, especially as contrasted to cooperatively or state-owned means of wealth." Dictionary.com

What does it mean in plain English?

In a capitalist system, businesses make money for the people who own them. In 1912 and even in 1945, these businesses were often owned by single families, which meant that most of the country's capital wealth was owned by a very small percentage of people. These are represented by the Birlings and the Crofts (who you remember are constructs, created to represent this).

Business owners are also shareholders. In a capitalist society, the rich buy shares in business, or a corporation. When that business makes a profit, this money is paid out to the shareholders, and is called a dividend.

The more shares you own, the more money you will receive through a dividend. So you can see, in most capitalist economies, the rich get richer, as their capital (what they own, in terms of money), earns more and more money through investment. In this way, the rich also tend to own the most land, as this also generates more profit through farming or building or rent.

What Does a Capitalist Society Look Like?

Why the play is still relevant to you today.

Britain's economy is a capitalist one. Even today, according to The Independent in 2016:

> "The richest 1 per cent of people in the UK own almost a quarter of the country's wealth, a new report has revealed.
>
> The huge levels of inequality in the UK were revealed in a detailed assessment that also showed the richest five per cent of people in the country own 44 per cent of all wealth."

People who support this capitalist system argue that in a capitalist economy everyone is motivated to work harder, because they get more money this way. People who earn more money, spend more money on goods and services which other people make and provide.

This means there are more jobs for people making the goods, or providing the services. This means the whole of society benefits – everyone has the potential to make more money, and so the standard of living keeps getting better.

It does not matter that the top 5% own nearly 50% of the wealth of the country, what matters is that you, let's say Jo or Joe Average, in the middle 50th percent of the population, have a lot more wealth than you would have in a socialist economy. Yes, they say, there would be far fewer millionaires and billionaires in a socialist economy, but that level of social equality is not much good if most people are poorer as a result.

Priestley argued against this in his play, in 1945. He would probably agree with this quotation in the Independent article, ""Globally, the richest one percent own more wealth than the rest of the world put together. This huge gap between rich and poor is undermining economies, destabilising societies and holding back the fight against poverty." Sally Copley, Oxfam's Head of UK Policy Programmes and Campaigns.

What's Inequality Like Now?
In The Guardian, Professor Dorling argues that this is the same level of inequality as we had in Britain in 1940, "The last time the best-off took as big a share of all income as they do today was in 1940, two years before the publication of the Beveridge Report, which became the basis of the UK's welfare state after The Second World War." The Guardian, June 27th, 2012.

What is Socialism?
"1. a theory or system of social organization that advocates the vesting of the ownership and control of the means of production and distribution, of capital, land, etc., in the community as a whole.

2. procedure or practice in accordance with this theory."
(Dictionary.com)

What does it mean in plain English?
The government owns as much of big business as possible – transport, railways, car manufacturing, house and road building, gas, electricity, telephones, coal, steel etc. The profits from these businesses go to the government. The government makes sure workers are paid fair wages, by paying them directly in these businesses.

But indirectly, everyone is paid, because the government spends all that they earn from these businesses on looking after the people – health, education, and welfare are free, so poverty is reduced. Essentials like water, electricity, gas, the telephone system, trains and buses are owned by the government so that prices are kept low and everyone pays the same for their services.

Although this means that there are still a lot of businesses not owned or run by the government, in a socialist economy their profits are normally taxed at a higher rate. This gives the government even more money to spend on social welfare, so everyone is looked after. It makes for a fairer society, because the poor are less poor, and the rich are less rich.

Why didn't society vote for socialism before 1945

Capitalists argue that much of this is inefficient. Yes, it does mean that everyone appears to get a fair share. However, with any business run by the government, workers know that the business will always stay afloat, in business. Consequently, they don't have an incentive to work more efficiently to make more profit. This makes the government-run businesses less profitable. What's the point of working harder or finding better ways to work, if none of the profits are going to come to you in wages?

This could mean that the government gets less tax from business. This would mean that the government gets less money to spend on services and the welfare state. Therefore, capitalists claim, most people will be worse off. Even though there is equality of pay in society, you make people more equal by making them poorer.

On the other hand, they argue, if the top 5% get very rich, that's just proof that the system is working and businesses are making large profits because they are so efficient.

Tricky to decide, isn't it?

As we have seen, Priestley is a socialist.

The Importance of Character's Names

Eva Smith

Eva is an allusion to Eve, as the mother of all humanity. It is the Latin form of Eve, so originally the same name. This matches Priestley's Christian message: if we are "members of one body", then we are all connected through our original mother, Eve. Eva's similarity to Eve draws this point out. It is also a name which exists in nearly every European language, and so again she symbolises every woman.

Smith, as the most common English surname, is chosen because it represents everyman – and that fits perfectly with the symbolism of Eve/Eva.

Of course, students often say, "no way Mr Salles, you are reading too much into this, he just chose the name Eva."

But I say, "Yes way". To find out why, let's leap into history.

The Census of 1911

(This is the last census available online, so I can't check 1945)

If we look at the record of everyone living in the UK in 1911, we can see how likely it is that Eva is just a name, or chosen for symbolic reasons.

If we search in London, we find only 504 'Eva Smith's. This is deliberate. Even though 'Smith' is such a common surname, Priestley is confident no one in his audience will know an 'Eva Smith' – this means they are much more likely to pick out its symbolic meaning.

To put these names in context, there were 27,765 Mary Smiths in 1911, and 21,467 Elizabeth Smiths.

Daisy Renton

Daisy is also a very rare name. There are only 1610 Daisy Smiths in the country in 1911. Again, this is another reason for us to see it as a symbolic name.

This is the only name in the play which is very new – women only began being named after flowers in the 19th century. Priestley's audience could see a link with her desire of "making a good fresh start", and the freshness of her name – we even say, 'fresh as a daisy'.

A "daisy" is vulnerable, innocent, a flower that can be easily be picked. Eric and Gerald pick her. A picked flower of course is chosen for its appearance, as she was. In this way, we can see how she is exploited for her looks. Even Sheila justifies getting her sacked because she looked so pretty, "But she was very pretty and looked as if she could take care of herself. I couldn't be sorry for her."

But, once removed from its roots, the flower dies. This is exactly what happens to Eva when she becomes Daisy. Eva has already lost her parents. As Daisy, she also loses the man she loves, Gerald.

Capitalism destroys workers' roots

This is symbolic of what capitalism is doing, taking people from their roots. Most female workers were born outside the city. Priestley's play argues that capitalism destroys them through cheap labour in factories, or underpaid city jobs. It is significant that Eva has no family to turn to. This also means that capitalism destroys their support network.

The census also tells us how typical this is. The 1911 census also reveals the proportion of women who have had to move to London to gain employment – a brief look at the census suggests about 9 in 20. The life expectancy is also low. The first two pages shows fifty women, and the oldest is 55.

If we look for Eva Smiths in Yorkshire (because that is where the invented Brumley is likely to be), we find 150. Only 3 of these are over 50. They are 53, 50 and 50. Workers really did die young.

If we look for a more common name, like Daisy in Yorkshire, where Priestley comes from and sets his play, we find that there are only 3 aged over 50 in the first 1000 listed on the census.

We can infer from this that Eva's and Daisy's suicide is not just a theatrical device to shock the Birlings. It is a perfect symbol of how life expectancy has been dramatically reduced by industrialisation, the terrible working conditions, the poor pay, the lack of a welfare state, and of course the lack of free health care.

Daisy Renton's are Incredibly Rare: Is she For Rent?

There are only three 'Daisy Renton's in the whole country, and none in London: it is incredibly rare. Renton is therefore even more obviously a symbolic name.

Eva will never earn enough to own her own home – she will always *rent on*. But more than this, once she loses the Milwards job, she is literally for rent.

At the Palace Bar, her continued descent toward prostitution would mean that her body was literally for rent. Gerald saves her from outright prostitution because "she looked young and fresh and charming and altogether out of place down here".

Again, we can see the symbolism at work in our expression 'fresh as a daisy'. She looks innocent, but this appearance also seems to be for rent.

Gerald literally rents her for the summer, until his friend returns. Indeed, if he wanted the relationship to continue, he would need to rent a property to put her in. She is, however, not even worth the price of rent to him, and he breaks off the relationship!

We can certainly argue that it would have been more expensive for Gerald to pay a prostitute for each time he has sex with Daisy, and that by keeping her rent free in the flat, she costs him very little.

It is important for Gerald not to see this. He desperately needs to present himself as a good man. Consequently, he does not want to see the relationship in these financial terms. Instead he claims, "I want you to understand that I didn't install her there so that I could make love to her."

However, his later actions show this to be a lie. Even his language shows he is lying to himself – we 'install' a possession, an object. This clearly symbolises how she is simply a possession he has rented for a few months, an object to be discarded when it has served its purpose.

If These are Priestley's Symbols, What Does Daisy's Name Symbolise to Eva – Why Does She Choose Daisy Renton?

She probably sees the same meanings as Priestley. Even though she won't want to admit to herself that her body is for rent, her unconscious tells her that she is.

She also sees herself as fragile, uprooted, and ready to be exploited.

However, in the name Daisy, there is an element of longing or hope: that she might remain beautiful, that her future might be bright, that she will maintain some innocence, never literally having to rent out her body for sex, as a prostitute.

Eric and Gerald both offer money without her asking – it is important that they maintain the illusion that this is not a financial arrangement. They are not paying for sex, their actions seem to say, they are just giving her money to get by.

These two names again show her dual purpose – as Eva, Priestley uses her to represent all workers. As Daisy, he uses her to represent all women who are sexually exploited by rich men.

Edna

Edna has almost nothing to say, although what she says is important, as you'll see. Her name is very close to Eva's – it is short, begins and ends with the same letters.

This echo and rhyme with Eva certainly suggests they are connected – they both symbolise the working classes. Edna is completely ignored by the Birlings, as a symbol of how little they care for the working classes.

There are 215,000 hits on the census for 1911 for Edna, showing how popular it was as a working-class name.

It is a name which comes to English from Ireland and Scotland, two countries historically invaded and oppressed by the English. Edna's name is therefore also symbolic of the oppression of the working classes by the rich.

The meaning in Gaelic, spoken originally in Ireland and Scotland, is 'kernel or grain'. Firstly, it symbolises something small and insignificant. This matches perfectly with the way she is viewed by the Birlings. Her lack of dialogue emphasises this.

But Priestley may also have in mind the association we have with these two words – in the phrases 'a kernel of truth', or 'a grain of truth'. Edna is needed in the play to link the truth, as shown by The Inspector, to the conditions and oppression of the working classes.

Probably to show how important she is, her first words are the play's title, "Please, sir, an inspector's called."

It's also significant that he chooses her to bring in The Inspector and, symbolically, to bring in the truth.

Eric

Eric's name is symbolic of rulers and violence, like Gerald's is. It is a Viking, Old Norse name. In England, Vikings have always been associated with violence. The name 'Eiríkr', combines two words, 'ei' – meaning 'ever, always' and 'ríkr' – 'ruler'.

We might interpret this to mean that Eric is not just descended from the ruling classes, but will always be a ruler, and by extension, will always be a capitalist. This would help explain why his learning of The Inspector's lesson isn't enough to prevent the second phone call. Priestley could be suggesting that Eric will forget the lesson, and revert to his earlier state, once the play is over. He will once again become part of the ruling classes, and sharing their behaviour towards the working classes.

There is one final possible piece of symbolism. Eric had stopped being a popular name once the Normans established control and rule, after 1066. It was revived in the 19th century after the publication of a children's novel, Eric, or Little by Little.

Priestley deliberately presents Eric as child-like. Eric himself tells us of Eva's description of him, "In a way, she treated me – as if I were a kid. Though I was nearly as old as she was." This is another hint that he won't be able to hold on to The Inspector's lesson – the influence of his parents will be too great. This is in complete contrast to his sister. Sheila tells her parents "And I'm not a child, don't forget", which implies that she will overcome her parents' influence by learning The Inspector's lesson.

Sheila
Sheila comes to English from the French, when the Normans conquered Britain in 1066. For several hundred years many of the ruling families took on French names, as well as speaking French.

Firstly, then, 'Sheila' is a symbol of her social superiority. It also links that superiority not just to wealth, but to oppression and conquest. This contrasts perfectly with Edna's symbolism of the oppressed or conquered Irish and Scottish.

The original Latin name that Sheila comes from is Cecilia. She is symbolic in two interesting ways. Cecilia is the feminine form of 'blind' in Latin. The educated audience, those who went to public schools and grammar schools, would all know this Latin, although we don't know how many would know the link between Sheila and Cecilia. However, Priestley certainly presents Sheila as blind to her actions at the start of the play, declaring "I couldn't be sorry for her" when she thinks about getting Eva sacked from Milwards.

However, The Inspector appears to completely change Sheila's view by the end of Act 2. This links to the second symbolic meaning. Saint Cecilia was a martyr, sentenced to death for refusing to worship Roman gods, instead worshipping the Christian God. For us, we see the parallel in her refusal to accept her parents view of their responsibility to the working classes – in effect she stops worshipping capitalism, and begins to see the truth of the need to be socialist, socially responsible, and remembering that we are all "one body".

Interestingly, her death at the hands of the Romans also symbolises Sheila's powerlessness. Because she is young, but even more because she is a woman, she has no real power within the ruling classes. This will be another reason for the second death – it may be that Sheila learning The Inspector's lesson is just not enough, as she won't have enough influence to change society. This is why her parents' views seem to influence the end of the play far more.

Gerald
Gerald is a fairly common name, with over 12,500 in London alone. However, it is, like Sheila's, a name that has come to Britain with the Normans, and is therefore symbolic of power and conquest, with the oppression of the working classes.

Unlike Sheila, it is not associated with a saint. Instead it is derived from the Germanic words for 'rule of the spear'. Here we can clearly see how his name is symbolic of oppression. It is also another way Priestley suggests that Gerald is more responsible for the death of Eva than many of the other characters. His is the only one associated directly with killing.

This is another clue that it is his male, sexual exploitation of Eva which is far worse than the exploitations of Arthur, Sheila and Sybil Birling.

Sybil
Sybil is also a name brought to Britain by the Normans, and so also symbolises power and oppression.

There is also a heavy irony involved in this name. Once again, much of Priestley's audience would have been educated at grammar schools and public schools. They would all know Greek mythology, and most would have learned some Greek alongside their Latin.

In Greek and Roman legend, there were ten sibyls, who were female prophets at different holy sites. They were revered, looked up to as having divine knowledge. This is so ironic to Priestley, because he deliberately portrays her has having so little knowledge:

- she does not know that Alderman Meggarty is a sexual predator
- she does not know that Eric is potentially alcoholic, (when Sheila and Gerald know about both)
- and of course she does not see, as Sheila does, that Eric must be the father of Eva's child
- finally, she does not see that denying charity to Eva was immoral

We can also see how her name is connected to Sheila's. Sheila's name alludes to blindness, but only she can see The Inspector's lesson fully. Sybil's name alludes to divine sight or knowledge, but she is blind to The Inspector's lesson and much else.

Arthur
The origin of the name is unknown. Therefore, it is universally associated with the legendary King Arthur. This obviously fits with Birling's position as head of the household. It also symbolises how families like the Birlings are in fact like kings: their collective power rules Britain – they control the wages of their workers, and also own so much of the country's wealth.

As with Sybil, Priestley also uses the name ironically. King Arthur was famous for defending Britain against oppressors, in the form of invading Angles and Saxons. Here, he is the oppressor, and The Inspector arrives to teach him the need to defend the country by defending the working classes.

Arthur was a king famous for promoting chivalry, an obligation on the part of the rich and powerful to respect and aid those most in need. It was particularly a code of behaviour which involved respecting women, and doing them no harm. We can see Priestley's heavy irony in the way Arthur treats Eva.

This is another reason why Priestley gives him the ironic line, "The Germans don't want war. Nobody wants war", so the audience know that Birling should have been thinking about the need to defend the country at this stage. It is the ruling classes' ignorance of the consequences of their actions that Priestley is suggesting lead directly to war two years later in 1914.

Alfred Tennyson, who you will probably remember wrote <u>The Charge of the Light Brigade</u>, wrote a book about King Arthur, <u>Idylls of the King</u>, which became hugely popular. Wikipedia states, "Arthur became a symbol of ideal manhood who ultimately failed, through human weakness, to establish a perfect kingdom on earth."

We can see the irony Priestley uses here, because Arthur Birling is clearly far from the ideal of manhood.

However, Arthur also strove to make England perfect, a better place. This is exactly what Priestley wants the ruling classes to do. He wants them to recognise the irony in Arthur's name as an irony in their own behaviour. When they realise this, he hopes they might change, vote Labour, and try to make England better.

Thanks Mr Salles, But Really, How Will I Use This in an Exam?
Well, any of this can and will suddenly come to you as you are writing about a character. Remember, the whole play is symbolic, so you should always write about the symbolic reasons for a character's name, if the question is about a character.

If the question is about a theme, or about the contrast between the older and younger generations, it is even more useful. These are some of the things you can write about confidently:

1. Arthur, Gerald, Sheila, Sybil and Eric all have names which come into the language through conquest, and are symbols of oppression.

2. Arthur and Eric are both named after rulers and kings, to make that link with capitalism and oppression really clear.

3. Arthur's name, and his wife's, Sibyl's, are both used ironically. This is because Priestley is satirising them, and attacking them for how far their behaviour is from the ideal. Ideal behaviour is alluded to in the origin of their names.

4. Priestley deliberately uses references to Greek and Latin language and mythology in his names, because he knows these are languages and allusion that the

powerful upper and upper middle classes will understand – they are the ones who have been to public school, and many to grammar schools. If he speaks to them in their own language, as it were, he increases the chance of their understanding his message.

5. Eva's name is clearly symbolic of how he wants us to view the working classes, as the mother of all of us. The whole of society collapses if the workers aren't there, so we should look after them.

6. Daisy's name is clearly symbolic of Eva's mental state and desires for escape, innocence, and new life.

7. Priestley links his message to Christian belief through Christian language – "We are members of one body. We are responsible for each other" - and links this to the Christian origin of his oppressed women, Eva and Sheila. In this way he asks that we all behave more like Sheila, in learning his lesson.

8. It is also a way in which he attacks the patriarchy: the two characters who are most associated with goodness (apart from The Inspector), are females – Eva and Sheila - who are both victims of male society, the patriarchy.

9. Eric's and Gerald's names are linked with violence – Eric as a Viking name, Gerald through etymology and 'rule of the spear' – and this symbolises how their actions towards Eva, in sexually exploiting her, are worse than the actions of the other characters.

10. The Inspector's name is a deliberate allusion to the ghosts of Dickens's <u>A Christmas Carol</u>. This points us to their similar didactic, moral purpose, in asking their audience to make what the authors see as correct moral choices in the way the rich behave towards the poor and the working classes. They are both texts demanding more social justice, and both share the same message of shared responsibility.

Choose a Theme Question if You Can

Any one of these ideas linked to the argument in your essay will force the examiner to consider giving you grades 7 and above.

However, if you have a choice between a character question and theme question, I hope you can see how much easier it is to make more of these points in the theme question. When you write about a theme, many of the points above will link in.

It is so much easier to write about Priestley's ideas when you write about a theme, and this always propels your essay into the top band.

What is the Exam Question Likely to be?

Of course, the exam board can ask you any question. But, because they want everyone to be able to answer, it is unlikely that you will get an unpredictable one. If we look back at every An Inspector Calls question set by AQA from 2011 to 2017, we find:

a) 1 Gender roles
b) 1 Eva
c) 1 The beginning
d) 2 The ending
e) 2 Birling
f) 2 The Inspector
g) 3 Eric
h) 3 Gerald
i) 3 Mrs Birling
j) 3 Class, Inequality, The Inspector's message about society
k) 4 Contrast and Conflict, Older generation v Younger Generation, Responsibility v Lack of Responsibility
l) 4 Sheila

In reality, every question, no matter what the wording, is basically the same:
"What is Priestley trying to get his audience to think and feel, and how does this help his audience in 1945 learn his feminist, socialist and anti-war message?"

If the question is just on one character, say Eric, then you will just ask yourself, "How does Priestley use Eric to portray his socialist message and his attack on the patriarchy?"

If the question is just on Mrs Birling, you will ask yourself, "How does Priestley use Mrs Birling to show the damaging effects of the patriarchy and capitalism on her and those she deals with, so that his audience learns his socialist message and attacks the patriarchy?"

In other words, all the questions are basically the same, you just draw slightly different evidence for all of them.

You can see that The Inspector's words will always be relevant to every question. You can also see that all the theme questions, those at a), j) and k) above are also the same: "What is Priestley trying to get his audience to think and feel, and how does this help his audience in 1945 learn his feminist, socialist and anti-war message?"

I'd also argue that the last of the really challenging questions, a) to d) above, was asked in 2014. It seems that the examiners really are determined to ask you very predictable questions. In order to get the highest marks, then, you need to prepare some unpredictable answers.

If you've already been taught this play at school, it is possible that you will find the feminist perspective, and the attack on the patriarchy, as a clear way in which your answers will be more original than others the examiner meets.

In Depth Understanding of the Characters

You are going to become an expert in each character, but you don't have to be. When you get to the end of the section on a character, ask yourself these questions:

1. What is the conventional interpretation of this character?
2. What alternative interpretation do I now think is more interesting or true?
3. How can I link this to how Priestley viewed society?
4. What two quotations do I need to prove each of the above?

This will give you the top six quotations to revise for each character, and that is much easier to remember than the whole guide.

Inspector Goole Explains the Whole of the Play

The Inspector in Act 1

The Inspector is a socialist, who believes that the profits of business should be used to improve the lives of ordinary men and women, either through higher wages, or government control.

The Inspector is a proxy for Priestley's views, but he is also the agent who drives the action of the play, not just a political figure.

The Inspector is An Ally of the Working Classes

A major part of the entertainment is in trying to work out who The Inspector is and how he appears to have access to secret knowledge. When he arrives, the lighting changes from "pink and intimate" to "brighter and harder". It is no longer rose tinted and innocent, but reveals the Birlings' and Gerald's guilt. This is The Inspector's purpose, to reveal the upper classes' guilt, not just to the audience, but to themselves so that they will have a chance to change their ways.

Edna introduces him: "he *says* his name's Inspector Goole", which implies that Edna may not believe he is a real inspector. Similarly, "he says it's important" also casts doubt on this.

This raises the possibility that who he says he is, and who he actually is are different. None of the upper-class characters realise this. Giving this undertone of doubt to Edna, the only working-class character, suggests that she is more perceptive.

However, if she does see that he may be an imposter, her words might hold out no hope that he will make a difference: "he *says* it's important" can be performed in a resigned way. This would imply she is so used to a life of subservience as a domestic servant that she is not able to appreciate The Inspector standing up for the rights of the working classes – her rights.

Alternatively, it can be performed in the opposite way, as a warning to the Birlings to listen to what he has to say, because "*he* says it's important" and he is the voice of authority.

Whichever interpretation you choose, it isn't a coincidence that Priestley decides that Edna should announce his presence. This allies him symbolically to the working class.

Priestley insists The Inspector must have an "impression of massiveness". This is because The Inspector is his proxy. When he has a "habit of looking hard" at people, he is behaving exactly as Priestley would, staring hard at the establishment and ruling classes, in order to accuse them.

The Inspector wants to shock, just as Priestley wants to shock his audience. The shock works as a theatrical experience, but also to get across his message – the upper classes damage lives. This is why he chooses to state that Eva has died a horrifically painful death: "Burnt her inside out, of course" … "She was in great agony". Concentrating on the pain forces the audience to be more affected by her death, and angrier at the cause of it: the characters on stage.

He emphasises this again: "Suicide of course". The curtailed sentences mimic her curtailed life. The throw away "of course" also shows how The Inspector suggests it is completely normal for a working-class girl to react this way – the implication being that the oppression of the upper classes leaves them no choice. He implies she is just a statistic among many suicides of working-class women.

Goole: What's in a Name?

The Inspector's name is a homophone for 'ghoul', or ghost, and there is a strong reminder of Dicken's <u>A Christmas Carol</u> here. Priestley is signposting not just that there may be a supernatural mystery in the play, but that it is didactic, carrying a moral message that the protagonists' behaviour must change.

It is important to realise that The Inspector does not know everything, and is not in full control of events. His interest in Gerald does not appear pre-planned, "I see. Mr Croft is going to marry Miss Sheila Birling… Then I'd prefer you to stay." He clearly doesn't know that Gerald has had any part in Eva's life.

Perhaps he needs to prevent this marriage. This will tie in with Priestley's purpose – if she does not marry him, there is a very strong chance that she will be able to change the future, because she has learned The Inspector's message. If she does marry him, whether she has learned the lesson is open to doubt, because she will be marrying a man who completely disagrees with The Inspector's teaching.

The Inspector is a Teacher of Morality

As you know, Priestley's father was a teacher. The Inspector wants to teach the Birlings that: "we were all responsible for everything that happened to everyone".

The Inspector is actually here to teach, not just to discover what has occurred. This is why when Birling objects, saying "how I choose to run my business" is not relevant, The Inspector replies "it might be", clearly signposting that this is a political play, looking at the morality of business.

One way he examines this exploitation in business is through the wages Eva and her colleagues are paid, defending their right to strike. "After all, it is better to ask for the Earth than to take it" observes The Inspector, implying that capitalism literally robs people of what should be theirs. The metaphor implies that capitalism is in effect a form of theft.

For this reason, he looks accusingly at each character even before he knows what they have done. His reaction so far strongly suggests that he does not know any specific crime committed by Gerald. However, he still "looks at Gerald, then at Eric, then at Sheila" because he knows that they will all have committed some crime. Why? Because they are part of the ruling classes – it is simply in their nature. This is why he replies to Birling's claim that they are "respectable citizens, not criminals" with scorn: "Sometimes there isn't much difference as you think."

However, by the end of act 2 we can be quite certain he already knew of Sheila and Eric's part in Eva's tragedy. The end of Act 2 also shows us that he knows Mrs Birling has denied Eva charity. Think about this. If he wanted to teach the Birlings his lesson, he would simply move through each of them in turn, as he does. Then he would deal with Gerald afterwards, if anything had come to light.

Power Tends to Corrupt

That he starts first with Gerald is visually significant. Remember, the audience has no idea who is responsible. But even before The Inspector accuses Birling, his most ominous message is about Gerald: "I see. Mr Croft is going to marry Miss Sheila Birling... Then I'd prefer you to stay." It tells the audience that he is most certain of Gerald, *even though he has no idea yet what Gerald has done.*

How can this be? It is because of how The Inspector and Priestley view the social hierarchy. He assumes that the most powerful will have had most power to abuse, and therefore that they will be the most likely to be corrupt and oppress the working classes, or indeed anyone socially inferior to themselves. It is another way in which Priestley suggests the ruling classes cannot be trusted.

This is why he looks at Sheila last: she is only a woman in a patriarchal society. And of course, this is exactly how power is used in the play – Gerald abuses his power over Sheila through his infidelity. Birling appears to abuse his son, keeping him in lowly paid work with little real responsibility. Sheila is only able to achieve any kind of independence through marriage.

It implies that Priestley believes we could confront any member of the ruling classes and find a similar abuse of power.

He Allies Himself with Women. Is he a Feminist?

There is a possibility that he is a bit of a feminist. The Inspector deliberately focuses on "these young women" killing themselves as though to suggest that they have a much worse experience, and are far more vulnerable to capitalist exploitation than men.

It helps, of course, that all the women in Priestley's audience can now vote, whereas in 1912, none of them had this right.

The Inspector teaches a feminist viewpoint. We should "put ourselves in the place of these young women counting their pennies". The lack of money emphasises his motive to highlight their exploitation – they are given so little in wages, that "pennies" are all that is left to save. They are literally at the "back" of the house because that is where the worst rooms are for rent. Symbolically, they are at the "back" because this is where they in the social hierarchy: inferior and marginalised.

Priestley focuses on women because they will be half of his audience. More importantly, this half can now vote. Even more importantly, millions of them have been in jobs only made possible by war and the absence of men. He needs to affect women most, because they have the most to lose if the country rejects socialism in the 1945 election. Consequently, he makes sure The Inspector is an ally to Eva and to Sheila.

Sheila reacts straight away to seeing the photograph. As she runs out, he stares "speculatively after her". This can't be because he wonders what she has done – he already knows this, which is why he showed the photograph to her in the first place. His speculation must be because he is wondering if he can now use her emotional guilt.

As a dramatic device, this raises the tension, but also suggests that Priestley is asking the same question of his audience – can he affect their emotions sufficiently so that they too will feel guilt or the weight of injustice enough to vote for a socialist government?

The Inspector Plays Down Sheila's Guilt

If we look logically at the tragedy of Eva's life, getting sacked by Birling was not the worst thing that could have happened to her. Indeed, we might suppose that the job at Millwards, a prestigious shop, without manual labour, and the noise and danger of the factory, is a considerable step up from working for the Birlings. Losing this job is far more costly, both personally (because she would prefer it to the Birlings' job), and because it led directly to Eva considering prostitution at The Palace Bar.

The Inspector calls her only "partly to blame", "just as your father is". There would be many capitalists and businessmen in the audience who would think Birling acted completely properly in getting rid of the ringleaders of the strike – their wage demands would significantly reduce profits.

By equating Sheila's greater fault with her father's action, The Inspector is trying to make Birling seem worse.

Alternatively, perhaps Birling's actions are much worse – his actions after all affect the whole of his workforce, thousands of Evas. Moreover, he had it in his power to actually make all of their lives better, by paying more – he had a greater gift, which he chooses not to give. Sheila, in contrast, has no power, and therefore has nothing she can give – she can only take away.

For this reason, The Inspector does not accuse her of being spiteful, cruel or thoughtless. These would be criticisms of her character and personality. Instead he presents her behaviour in terms of the exploitation of power: it's "the power you had". To emphasise this socialist point, he hammers home the emotional message when Sheila would like to turn back time: "but you can't. It's too late. She's dead". Priestley deliberately gives The Inspector these short sentences to emphasise the finality of what she has done.

He is Like a Supernatural Apparition

Birling's own words have invoked his presence, as though The Inspector is supernatural. Birling's expression of the capitalist view, "that a man has to mind his own business, and look after himself and his own" summon The Inspector, to challenge this capitalist belief.

Looked at from this perspective, the death of Eva isn't necessarily why he arrives. Instead it suggests that the death happens at the same time as The Inspector arrives. It is as though the arrival and the death are only a potential future. Only when Birling utters those words, does that future happen. The Inspector arrives to contradict those very words. It is to teach his socialist lesson.

This is why Priestley stages the doorbell ring as an interruption. In case the audience miss the importance of this, he makes sure Sheila refers back to it, "Is that when The Inspector came, just after father had said that?" Again, Priestley is pointing out that the idea that "man has to mind his own business" is the most corrupt one, much more corrupt than capitalism alone.

If you think about this, it is a logical point of view for Priestley to take. If he wants to persuade people to change their minds, he won't persuade business men to pay much higher wages, and he won't persuade those who have inherited their wealth to give up being capitalists. However, he can persuade them all to think it would be better to think as much of their fellow human beings, man and woman, as they do of their own family. Especially as that would also be the Christian thing to do.

The Inspector in Act 2

The Inspector is Not Fully in Control

It is important in the staging for the audience to see that The Inspector is not in full control. It is dramatically more satisfying if we can also see him surprised, and it helps with the mystery he is setting up in his Whodunnit genre – who is The Inspector really?

For this reason, Priestley does not want to keep Sheila on stage: "_Inspector_: well, I don't want to keep you here. I've no more questions to ask you." This implies that he did not expect to have such an influence on her. Perhaps more importantly, it suggests that any such influence won't be enough to change the future.

Perhaps he doesn't want to keep Sheila there, as she holds less power. He is attacking the patriarchy, so he really needs time to deal with the men in the household, without women present.

This is interesting. We can see as the third act develops that it is Sheila who tries to make her parents and Gerald learn The Inspector's lesson. Yet, in the early stages of the play, he simply dismisses her. It can't be because he is sexist, as this would work against Priestley's message to the crucial women voters in his audience.

But another reason is that it makes the play dramatically more interesting. It means The Inspector is taken by surprise. He knows that he might influence Sheila profoundly: "We often do (have an influence) on the young ones". But he doesn't know that she will understand him so well. Once he sees that she thinks like he does, particularly in helping to expose Gerald, he is keen for her to stay.

The Inspector is Supernatural

This quotation also tells the audience that The Inspector is probably supernatural – a real inspector or a fraud would not say this. Alternatively, it is the kind of wording a teacher would use – so he could be cast in the role of teacher. His job is to break down walls, "and it will be all the worse when he does" as Sheila observes, thinking like he does. This adds to The Inspector's dramatic role. Of course, the supernatural role, and the role of the teacher are one and the same in A Christmas Carol, and Priestley probably intends them to be the same here.

Priestley also plants a further supernatural idea, with The Inspector's involvement in Eva's death. This is revealed by his instruction, "if there's nothing else we'll have to share our guilt." This opens up the possibility that he too feels guilty.

Some readers therefore imagine that there may be some supernatural complicity in Eva's death, otherwise he wouldn't feel guilt. In other words, as a God-like figure, he holds her life in the balance, and only decides to kill her when the family don't "share our guilt". This appears to be a ruthless interpretation, but even Christians would accept that this is exactly how God must work. This is why good people die all the time, for reasons we cannot fathom – it is simply that God's will is unknowable.

For example, if she has not yet died, and her death depends on the family sharing their guilt, this means that they could save her by learning The Inspector's lesson, just as Scrooge changes the future shown to him by the Ghost of Christmas Yet to Come, simply by learning to be responsible for others.

Priestley was obsessed with time, and believed that people could sense the future. He explores this dramatically in many of his plays. Here characters never use knowledge about the future to gain a personal advantage – no one buys shares in companies they know will prosper, no one has a winning lottery ticket with numbers they know will come up – instead, characters learn that they can alter the future for the benefit of others. It allows them to change their present behaviour to bring about a better future for society. In fact, he wrote a whole book about this, <u>Man and Time</u>, in 1964.

Schrödinger's Cat
The idea that possible futures are equally balanced, awaiting a particular cause is also one that Priestley became familiar with through quantum physics. Schrödinger, a famous physicist dramatised this in 1935, with a thought experiment involving a cat locked in a steel box for one hour. In the cage is a phial of acid. Its trigger is an atomic particle. When it decays, it will trigger the phial to release the acid, which will kill the cat. This decay may happen within the one hour, or it may not.

At the quantum level, the particle is both a particle and a wave, and only decides on which state when it is observed. In the thought experiment the cat is therefore alive – because the particle is in fact a wave, but also dead, because the wave is in fact a particle. *You determine its state when you open the box and observe it – only at that moment is the cat alive or dead, one or the other, and not both.*

This is a very close parallel with Eva – she is both alive and dead until the moment the Birlings and Gerald observe her. If they decide they caused her tragedy, she lives. If they decide they are blameless, she dies. Priestley is also probably attracted by the timeline involved in the thought experiment – acts 2 and 3, when the characters decide on their level of blame, will take about 1 hour on stage.

The advantage of this interpretation is that it does not present God as cruel. We would think it very cruel for God to kill Eva simply in order to teach the Birlings a lesson about social responsibility. However, if God is like quantum physics, the problem of cruelty disappears – Eva is both alive and dead at the same moment – only the Birlings' viewpoint determines which state she remains in. In order to make sense of this argument, you need to see The Inspector as having the same supernatural powers as God.

The Inspector Attacks the Class System
Mrs Birling accuses him of being 'impertinent'. She is absolutely correct: his job is to question the class system.

Priestley gives Sheila violent imagery to describe this questioning; "so that we'll hang ourselves". This violent metaphor reveals Priestley's anger – hanging is a punishment for murder. He accuses the capitalist system of committing the equivalent crime – of murdering its workers.

His "duty" is to expose the lies of the Birlings to themselves – this is the only way they will change their behaviour.

It is important that Priestley does not give this anger to The Inspector, who barely raises his voice in the play. Instead he gives this anger to the younger Birlings – Eric and Sheila. However, because anger alone will not persuade his audience, Priestley needs to encourage empathy in his audience. Only when they can feel the injustice and suffering of the working classes, like Eva, can they begin to change their behaviour.

Consequently, he is not all powerful. Priestley doesn't wrap things up like a true morality play – goodness does not triumph over evil. Instead, like a teacher, The Inspector can only present Priestley's lesson, he can't make the characters act on it. He tells Mrs Birling "I think you did something terribly wrong", but this presupposes that she might not think that. And this foreshadows her rejection of his lesson.

Sensing this, that her sense of superiority will not permit her to feel guilt, he appeals to her feelings as a woman and mother, "she was here alone, friendless, almost penniless, desperate. She needed not only money but advice, sympathy, friendliness. You've had children. You must have known what she was feeling." The listing in triplets reveals how he is trying to appeal to her emotions. But the appeal fails, perhaps because she never was that sort of mother.

Perhaps Priestley is suggesting other upper-class mothers are also devoid of feeling. In Priestley's time, they gave up their children, sending them away to boarding school from the age of 7 if they were a son. They were trained to be less empathetic to their children. Upper class girls, however, were far more attached to their mothers, as in 1910 only about 5000 girls attended Public schools. This is probably why Priestley finds it easier to make Sheila most likely to empathise with Eva. We might argue that Eric only empathises with her so much because she is the mother of his child.

Faced with Sibyl's resistance, The Inspector's language becomes ever more violent. But this also might betray a sense that he knows he will not get through to her, just as Priestley knows that the upper classes did not learn the lesson of World War One: "you slammed the door in her face...why didn't...I'm not asking you... I want to know...why didn't...I warn you..."

He has cleverly planned to get her to admit that she is not sorry, "you're not even sorry now" and he knows that she will then blame the father of the unborn child. We can be reasonably certain here that at this point he already knows it is Eric's child: "who is to blame then?"

(It is structurally important that Eric is not present at this stage. Eric's absence is unexplained. However, his first words at the beginning Act 3 give a strong clue to where he has been. He asks, "You know, don't you?" referring to his fathering Eva's child. This strongly suggests that he has been out to look for Eva. We can also infer that he has not found her, because in Act 3 he believes she has committed suicide).

The Inspector in Act 3

Good v Evil

A didactic morality play would keep The Inspector on the stage to teach his lesson right up to the end. Similarly, so would a detective, Whodunit play, where The Inspector would reveal everything at the end.

Again, it is very interesting that Priestley rejects both these conventions of the two genres he has borrowed from. He also rejects the tidy, happy-ever-after resolution of A Christmas Carol. Why?

One possibility is that he is making a point about real life. His audience, who have just seen millions killed in The Second World War, are not so likely to believe in happy endings. With hundreds of thousands of soldiers returning from war, he knows they are also likely to have killed fellow men, even women and children. The binary good versus evil structure of a morality play would also not feel anything like real life. Consequently, Priestley deliberately leaves us with ambiguity – are Gerald and Eric more good than evil? Will Sheila's sense of injustice last?

Priestley and God

Another possibility is a subversion of the idea of God. In Christian belief, death is when life finally makes sense – the good go to heaven, and the sinners and non-Christians go to hell. Priestley attacks this view. The death at the end does not make sense – it is deliberately ambiguous. Moreover, if Eva has committed suicide, she has committed a mortal sin, and will go to hell. Even though the audience see her as a victim, God will not.

This is very important to Priestley, because of his political message. This says that waiting for God to act is useless. The power to change society and the fate of the people in it rests with people living right now. If he needs people to act, to vote Labour, to prevent future war, then he needs them to believe their actions really matter.

This is another reason why The Inspector chooses to leave. Priestley needs to show his characters making up their own minds, as that is what he wants his audience to do. They have to mimic what his characters are doing, so he can't just have The Inspector permanently on stage proving the characters are guilty and wrong.

He knows that the characters won't all heed his message, but he hopes that the audience will. For Priestley, then, it is Eric and Sheila's words he wants the audience to hear. But he also needs their scepticism about what they hear, because the whole audience know that any change in 1912 amounted to nothing by 1939. The country made the same mistake twice, fighting two world wars. This is reinforced by the second death of Eva.

Priestley and Genesis

Here Priestley and the Christian God face similar problems. If God exists outside time, he can see how all our lives will develop and end. This is just like the playwright and his characters. However, for life to have meaning for people, as well as characters, they have to believe their choices matter. This is why God does not simply create Adam and Eve as perfect, living happily ever after in Eden. Instead, he engineers a choice.

If Adam and Eve choose to do exactly as God says, they will live forever. In Eden, God places two trees, "the tree of life" and "the tree of knowledge of good and evil". He only forbids them to eat the fruit of one tree: "But of the tree of the knowledge of good and evil, thou shalt not eat of it: for in the day that thou eatest thereof thou shalt surely die."

God deliberately gives Adam and Eve free will, to give them the opportunity not to listen to him. Priestley dramatises exactly the same thing, giving his characters the opportunity to listen to The Inspector, or to choose to ignore him.

Just as God then withdraws, and allows Adam and Eve to act independently, so does The Inspector. This is why Priestley removes him during Act 3. Of course, he isn't just doing this because he has Genesis in mind. He is doing it to point out to his audience that their free will is what most matters – he wants them to exercise it by voting Labour. For a modern audience, he wants us to keep choosing social responsibility, rather than merely looking after our "own".

The Inspector Exposes Eric and Capitalists as Thieves
For example, Eric's drinking makes us question Eric's apparent following of The Inspector's message – he does this while drunk. What will he think when he is sober? Will he still follow The Inspector's teaching then?

The exchange with Eric exposes him. First, The Inspector asks if they met "by appointment", implying that this was a business transaction – money for sex. When Eric says no, The Inspector asks, "More drinks?" implying that he exploited her even more than with a financial arrangement –he simply got her drunk so that she would not refuse him. This is also far cheaper than paying for sex.

The Inspector's words, though not his manner, are incredibly angry. "But you took her home again?" places an emphasis on "took", implying that Eric treated her as a possession. This is mirrored by the irony of "And you made love again?" Because Eric has already confessed that the first time was anything but love, and most probably rape.

It is interesting that The Inspector is not more explicit here – he never accuses Eric of rape, nor does he accuse him of simply exploiting Eva for sex. Perhaps it is because he is leading Eric to admit to the only provable crime of the play, stealing £50 from his father's business.

When Eric admits she knew "I didn't love her" The Inspector subtly accuses him of not asking her to marry him anyway. This is why he uses the word "propose" instead of 'suggest' or 'decide': "So what did you propose to do?"

£50 is nearly a year's salary that Eric has given Eva – this suggests that Eric has been pocketing the money – he can't possibly have been giving her all that money in the few months they are together, if she needed to go to Mrs Birling's charity.

Again, Priestley does this on purpose, to get his audience to question Eric. It is the kind of detail which would trouble a contemporary audience after the play. They would see that the sums just don't add up, in a way which is very difficult for a modern audience.

Why doesn't The Inspector pick up on this and accuse Eric of lying, taking most of the money for himself? Probably because he wants his audience to think hard, and draw conclusions for themselves. This is also much more likely given the apparent genre of the play as a "Whodunit". Priestley's cunning is to set this up so that the audience leave knowing not just who is responsible for Eva's death, but who is responsible for the two world wars: a capitalist patriarchy.

This is why The Inspector accuses him of theft, "You stole the money", Eric refuses to accept this responsibility: "Not really". It symbolises how capitalists are criminals.

Eric Represents the Patriarchy of 1945 (When he Would be in his Fifties and in Power)
He needs to save Eric's crime last as it is only he, as the male, who will inherit Birling's business. So, if he wants to influence the future, he needs to influence Eric. We might argue, however, that if The Inspector can predict the future (and his closing speech certainly suggests he can predict World War One) he knows that Eric won't change his mind. If this is the case, then exposing Eric in this way is to remind the audience that the ruling classes are still feeling a lack of guilt in 1945. They steal from the workers they exploit, but they refuse to see it as theft.

Conservative Versus Labour
When the Inspector says, "I haven't much time", the words make no sense in context – a real police investigation would not require this urgency. This suggests his supernatural powers – he somehow knows that Gerald will expose him as not the real inspector, or he knows that the death of Eva is still pending, contingent on them being able to "divide the responsibility between" them.

However, to the audience at this moment in the play The Inspector's words will appear as very odd. Because they make no sense in the mouth of a real detective, they introduce a new level of suspense. They mean that, when Gerald returns, we are much more likely to believe that he was in fact "a hoax". It also introduces a note of desperation to The Inspector. Remember that historically Priestley, like nearly everyone else in the country, did not expect the country to vote for a Labour government. He is more desperate because he knows how unlikely this is. This desperation is reflected in The Inspector's final words.

Is there a sense of desperation when he says to them "But each of you helped to kill her…Remember…Remember…Remember what you did"? Does he already suspect, not just that they won't feel guilty, but that they will actually forget what part they played entirely? This is akin to the country forgetting about the deaths of World War One. It is also like what he fears, the country ignoring the deaths of World War Two.

In order to remind his audience of these deaths, before he leaves, The Inspector suggests that he already knows war is coming and that Eric will die in it: "And now she'll make you pay a heavier price still" can only mean that Eric's death is the price the Birling parents will pay.

The Inspector's Last Words
The Inspector uses biblical language, "We are members of one body", which you remember comes from the Anglican communion, and helps Priestley's audience equate The Inspector's socialist message with Jesus' Christian message. "We are responsible for each other" is the next part of the speech – the socialist message grafted directly on to the Christian one. By allying the language of the church to the language of socialism, he suggests that socialism is a moral duty, almost a religious duty.

Because he realises that Britain is still a patriarchal society in 1945, though less so now than in 1912 (because in 1945 women can vote) he warns "if **men** will not learn that lesson". This emphasis on "men" asks all the women in the audience to seize power through their vote, in contrast to the "men" who have led them to two world wars: "then they will be taught it in fire and blood and anguish."

Here Priestley is being didactic. However, because The Inspector is speaking in 1912, we understand that his powers are supernatural – he has foreseen the wars that the audience have lived through. It is another way in which Priestley hints at The Inspector's supernatural powers.

Priestley decides that Sheila should make this connection. Eric points out that The Inspector first arrived when Birling was attacking social responsibility, and socialists as "cranks". But only Sheila appreciates the supernatural significance of this: "Sheila: (sharply attentive) Is that when The Inspector came, just after father had said that?... It's queer – very queer ... was he really a police inspector?"

He contrasts this with Birling's reaction about The Inspector, "Probably a socialist or some sort of crank". Birling's judgment has been fatally undermined at the beginning with his pronouncements on war and The Titanic. So, Priestley implies that Birling is correct in deciding that The Inspector is "a socialist" but wrong to dismiss this as "a crank". In this way he invites his audience to think again about socialists and voting Labour.

The final words spoken about him are again from Sheila. She proves that it makes no difference that there may have been five different girls, and it makes no difference if none of them committed suicide. What matters is "you began to learn something".

In this way Priestley shows that The Inspector's most important role has been that of a teacher. Her final words about him repeat his final words, "Fire and blood and anguish". This is crucial to Priestley, because it tells his audience that his socialist message won't just save the "millions" of "John Smiths" and "Eva Smiths" from exploitation, it will save them from future wars.

Eric Birling

Eric in Act One

Eric and Gerald Keep Each Other's Secrets

The most obvious mystery about Eric is why, in his early twenties, he is already an alcoholic. One possible reason for his drinking is the hypocrisy of his family, and symbolically Priestley uses this to show his disgust at the hypocrisy of the ruling classes. Eric first "suddenly guffaws" when Gerald tells Sheila that he will "be careful", after she has told him that she is suspicious of Gerald's time away from her in the summer.

This very strongly suggests that Eric knows exactly what Gerald has been doing, being unfaithful with Daisy. It may even suggest that he knows that the woman he has got pregnant is the same one Gerald had the affair with.

There is an undertone suggesting that Gerald, as Eric's social superior, and the more economically powerful male, behaves as a dominant male in a herd. Gerald would have the sexual relationship first, and Eric would only be allowed to step in afterwards. Looked at in this way, the males in the play behave no differently from animals.

This is also an attack on the patriarchy and sexism of the time. Eric is siding with Gerald's infidelity here, rather than revealing it to his own sister – this is symbolic of how unimportant women are to the men in the world of this play and in the world Priestley is attacking.

Alternatively, we might believe that Eric has no knowledge of Eva's past when he has a relationship with her. This would mean his sudden "guffaw" indicates he simply knows that Gerald is routinely unfaithful. It is simply a habit with him. Eric would certainly see this first hand as they both attend the Palace Bar specifically with the intention of picking up women or prostitutes.

Eric is also at the centre of the mystery of the play. Priestley portrays him from the beginning as deliberately withholding information, so that the audience knows he has something to hide. When Birling discusses women's clothing as a "token of their self respect" Eric replies "(eagerly) Yes, I remember" before cutting himself off. Priestley wants us to infer his secrecy concerns a woman, before we find out the family are implicated in Eva's suicide.

This is amplified when Gerald jokes about his knighthood being offered so long as there is no family scandal, "Unless Eric's been up to something". Eric is made to respond "uneasily, sharply" so that we can see he has something scandalous to hide.

This might also be a show of power between Gerald and Eric. This again suggests that Gerald also knows that Eric is promiscuous, and may also imply that he knows he is in a relationship with Eva. We can see this joke as Gerald's reaction to Eric's disdain – it is a warning to Eric not to reveal this infidelity to Sheila, or he will reveal something damaging to Mr Birling about Eric.

This is why, when Gerald returns in Act 3, Eric doesn't bother telling him about his relationship with Eva. He knows Gerald must already know this. Instead, he tells him "I stole some money, Gerald, you might as well know", while in the same speech claiming that the "important thing" is the death of the girl. Gerald must therefore know about Eric's relationship with Eva already.

Now we realise that taking Gerald out of the house is not just a useful plot device to allow him to expose The Inspector as a hoax. It also reveals how corrupt he is in maintaining Eric's secrets. In this way, Priestley suggests that the younger men will never truly learn The Inspector's lesson.

Does Eric Learn the Inspector's Lesson?
Priestley also uses Eric to comment on the action. He wants us to associate The Inspector's arrival with the advice Birling offers, and which the whole play attacks: "as you were saying, dad, a man has to look after himself". This also suggests that Eric is in a heightened state of alert, not drunk at all yet. He seems to unconsciously grasp that The Inspector arrives at this very moment precisely because of Birling's words and beliefs. Eric voices Priestley's own views. We call this being a proxy for Priestley.

Perhaps Priestley gives his views to such a flawed character (Eric is an alcoholic, a womaniser, possibly a rapist, and a thief after all) because he wants to show that everyone can change their views, and choose to do what is morally right: vote Labour, bring about a socialist future and care for the working classes.

Another possibility is autobiographical. Priestley had many affairs. By suggesting that Eric is still a good man, he is also suggesting that he is too. This would be Priestley's unconscious way of forgiving himself for being unfaithful.

Consequently, he uses Eric to attack Birling's capitalist views. He points out that paying low wages is unfair when the underpaid women "can't go and work somewhere else". This is because the factory owners operate a cartel (which is illegal). It means they can set the same low wages across all their businesses. If different employers paid more, then workers would be able to move for better wages, and so the free market would determine that all workers got higher salaries. Instead, Birling and the Crofts ensure that wages are kept artificially low in the cartel.

As he points out, "Why shouldn't they try for higher wages?" Eric's argument isn't simple socialism – he means that the capitalist system ought to be fair to both employers and employees. "We try for the highest possible prices" is therefore fair so long as workers are also allowed to ask for higher wages. He calls for a moral kind of capitalism, pointing out to Birling, "You said yourself she was a good worker", implying that she should be financially rewarded for this.

Will Eric Live Up to The Inspector's Lesson After 1912?
This also lays the ground for Eric's moral conflict. Perhaps he has become an alcoholic because he feels trapped in a family which has such an immoral head. Eric has had an

Oxbridge education, but his degree from one of the top universities in the country has counted for nothing within his family.

He is still made to learn the business form a very junior position. Priestley might also be pointing out Eric's cowardice here – with his education he ought to be able to forge a career away from home. However, he chooses to return to his parents, which appears so humiliating that he turns to alcohol and theft.

This weakness in him is a strong clue that he will not act on The Inspector's lesson, even though he wholly agrees with it. At the end of the play we will see that he defends The Inspector, but actually gives in to his father's demands. Actions speak louder than words.

Of course, the other possibility is that Priestley wants his audience to believe that Eric won't act on this teaching because he can't – The First World War will kill him, as it did so many of his generation.

Eric in Act Three

Eric's Confession as an Attack on the Power of Upper Class Men (The Patriarchy)
Eric is clearly experienced with prostitutes, which is why Eva "wasn't the usual sort". "Usual" implies visiting prostitutes is a habit for Eric. "She didn't know what to do" implies both that he is attracted to Eva's innocence, and also that he might realise that she is a woman he can exploit because of her ignorance.

Priestley presents this as a conflict in Eric because he wants us to be uncertain about Eric's motives. In his portrayal of men, it is quite possible to see an attack on masculine behaviour, and on the patriarchy.

Eric went to Eva's lodgings on the night he met her, "I insisted – it seems". "insisted" reveals that this may have involved physical force, and "it seems" shows how he has tried to forget his part in this, and distance himself from his guilt.

Priestley here is laying the ground for the possibility that Eric has raped Eva. She has tried to refuse him, "she told me she didn't want me to go in" but he overpowered this objection. He describes himself now as "in that state when a chap easily turns nasty". This will repay a lot of language analysis! First, he does not call it "a state". This suggests that this "nasty" state is one common to all men, not just to Eric: "that" implies we should all recognise it.

Then he distances himself from this nastiness, by referring to himself as "a chap", rather than 'I'. This is his attempt not to accept responsibility for forcing Eva to have sex with him. But it also reveals his view, and perhaps Priestley's, of how men behave – all men are capable of doing this, and many of them do. It is just them being chaps. Calling such violence the act of "a chap" also tries to diminish it, suggesting that although it is morally wrong, it is still excusable. This is a powerful clue that he knows there is no excuse for what he has done.

Eric further suggests this with his violent choice of language, "I threatened", and then he diminishes this again with "a row", a very euphemistic way to talk about demanding entry to her lodgings.

Does Eric Rape Eva?

We can read this as only demanding entry to her room. However, his language suggests that he has actually raped her. This is why he says, "And that's when it happened". Refusing to name what has happened strongly implies it is a word he needs to avoid. That word could well be rape. The use of the passive voice, "it happened" instead of the active 'And that's when I did it' is also a way for him to distance himself from what he has done.

He later calls "it" "stupid", again, refusing to name his act. His final act of distancing is to claim that he was too drunk to "even remember" what he had done. "I couldn't remember her name or where she lived" suggests that he really was very drunk, and perhaps chooses to be drunk on purpose. Being drunk, he can behave in immoral ways without the inconvenience of guilt. He only feels guilty when Eva tells him what he has done, but can pretend that "It was all very vague".

Priestley also gives Eric specifically Christian word choices here. Being unable to remember is "the hellish thing" and he immediately calls for help: "my God!". These choices clearly signal that he knows he has not just been cruel, but has committed a much more serious sin.

However, he clearly goes looking for her again, remembering enough to seek her out at the Palace bar. Again, he distances himself from this deliberate decision, with the passive voice "I happened to see her again in the palace bar".

A further clue that the first encounter was rape is given in his description of their second time having sex, "and this time we talked a bit". This strongly implies that there was no talk last time; he simply insisted on having sex, and Eva felt unable to refuse.

Eric's Sexual Exploitation of Eva is a Metaphor for Wider Exploitation of Women

This will also act as a metaphor, or an allegory, for what is happening to these women in the factories. They are exploited there, at the mercy of powerful men, who can artificially depress their wages, and use their power to sack them even when they are a "good worker".

This incident also reminds us of Eva's choice of suicide. She decides to metaphorically cleanse herself, specifically from the inside. She doesn't just kill herself as an act of despair, she attacks the parts of herself which have been touched by Eric. Possibly the most horrible aspect of this is the immediate effect on the baby. The Inspector is keen to point out the use of bleach burned out Eva's insides – the baby itself is also disgusting to Eva, and she wants to be cleansed of it. This further suggests how far she despises what

Eric has done to her, and is probably the most damning evidence that he has raped her, hence her disgust with her own unborn child.

So why did she let him back to her flat? Here we realise that she was not paid the first time they had sex – there has been no financial promise. She is so poor that she is willing to allow Eric back on the off chance that this will lead to some sort of financial security. He tells her "my name and what I did" so she immediately knows that she can at least track him down if she needs to. This also allows her not to view herself as a prostitute. She hasn't charged him for sex, so he has simply stolen it. The irony here is that actually she would have been financially better off is she had charged him.

Is Eric a Feminist Construct, So Women Will Vote Against Capitalism?
We can see Eric as a feminist construct, an average man, to suggest what the average man is capable of this sexual exploitation of women. This is echoed by what his father's "respectable friends" do with "these fat old tarts round the town".

This language reveals how much Eric hates the hypocrisy of his society and his father's generation. But his use of the phrase "I hate these fat old tarts" also reveals his disgust at his own hypocrisy in frequenting the Palace Bar, looking for sex. Again Priestley suggests, through Eric, that all men are disposed to pay for sex – indeed the more privileged they are, the more they seem to feel entitled. This is also the point of giving Sheila the story about councillor Meggarty assaulting a friend of hers. His anger at himself for being a hypocrite also gives us a reason for his drinking.

The Necessary Illusion That Eva is not a Prostitute
He admits Eva "treated me – as if I were a kid". This is in response to his naïve assumption that they should get married. On the one hand this could be because, as Eric says, "I didn't love her". But on the other hand, Eva knows that the son of Arthur Birling would never be allowed to marry so far beneath his social class.

For this reason, she refuses to get a job, and Eric "insisted on giving her enough money to keep her going". Her adult perspective is therefore to get him to pay for her, without demanding money. In this way, she can have sex with him for money, but allow them both not to see it as a financial arrangement for sex. However, her suicide strongly suggests that she is not really able to enter into this illusion, and finds herself too disgusting to live.

In some ways Gerald's treatment of Eva has been far worse. He has simply dismissed her. Eric has stood by her as best he can, even if she does not believe they could ever be married. Could Priestley be asking all his upper-class female audience members to look again at their own marriages – are they so very different from the financial arrangements made by Gerald and Eric with Eva? The only real difference appears to be that they can claim their husbands loved them. Other than that, they were still kept financially by their husbands, and not allowed or required to work.

This is in stark contrast to the women watching the play in 1945. They would be far more likely to rebel against this patriarchal exploitation of women, as they would be far more likely to have worked during the war. Priestley could therefore be fuelling women's resentment of men. They would want to reject this patriarchal society and, according to the play, the best hope for that is to vote for a socialist party.

Eric Probably Won't Live by The Inspector's Teaching

Priestley also wants us to be angry at Eric's refusal to take real responsibility so far. Eric says he has given Eva "about fifty pounds all told". One pound was made up of 20 shillings. 50 pounds is therefore 1000 shillings. At 25 shillings a week, that's 40 weeks' earnings. Considering his relationship with Eva can't have lasted longer than November to April, 26 weeks, two possibilities present themselves. Firstly, Eva is charging Eric about double what she would have earned in work. Or secondly, Eric is using the extra money on his own drinking.

Priestley deliberately leaves us in doubt about this. He wants us to be critical of Eric, because he represents the hypocrisy of upper-class men. They exploit women by forcing them to consider selling their principles for financial security. This will be very relevant when we consider how society expects Sheila to put up with her husband's infidelity, and why she doesn't end the play refusing to ever be engaged with Gerald.

Priestley also lays the ground for us to judge Eric harshly, and to realise that he is the type of person not to accept ultimate responsibility for Eva's death. In other words, he is the kind of person not to act on The Inspector's teaching. For this reason, Eric doesn't see the money he has taken from his father's business as stealing, it is "not really" stealing as he intended to pay it back. This could be another reason that Priestley makes the sum so large – the audience will know that he won't be able to pay back such a large sum. They will know he is just deceiving himself.

Even the money he steals for Eva might be Priestley's attack on Eric. He is with Eva for only a few months, and yet he has stolen £50. As we've seen, this is much more than he would need to give Eva. Is he therefore using her as an excuse to steal from his father? If so, Priestley is not suggesting this is a theft with moral purpose, to help Eva and his unborn child. Instead, it suggests Eric is already corrupt, and therefore highly unlikely to retain The Inspector's lesson, even though he may want to. Self-interest and immaturity will get the better of him, and he won't be able to hang on to The Inspector's socialist ideal.

Does Priestley Want us to Agree with Eric?

Priestley probably wants us to sympathise with Eric. He accuses his mother: "you killed her – and the child…your own grandchild". It is Mrs Birling's snobbery that has allowed her to do this, her ability to see the working classes as not quite real people.

But at the same time, this is an immature response. The Inspector has spent a long time trying to tell each of the Birlings they are jointly responsible. By simply blaming his mother, "you killed her", Eric is trying to absolve himself from blame.

Eric's next lines might also undermine him – "You don't understand anything. You never did. You never even tried". It is almost a parody of the kind of sweeping statements we might expect a teenager to use in an argument with their parents.

However, Priestley takes a different tack, because he gives Birling this objection, "Why you hysterical young fool". Because Birling is already discredited, perhaps Priestley wants us to see Eric's words as a justifiable accusation. Perhaps Priestley wants us too to see Mrs Birling as a murderer.

On the other hand, if we take Eric's hatred of his parents as a proxy for Priestley's view, Priestley wants us to see that, however bad Eric is, his parents are even worse. This matters to him, because he is now writing for a younger generation in 1945, who he hopes will feel as Sheila and Eric do, and identify with them.

But, in a subtler way, he is also addressing those in his audience who were contemporaries of Sheila and Eric, who were around twenty-four in the outbreak of The First World War and who have not, in Priestley's eyes, learned their lesson. He wants them to feel guilt that their past was much like Eric's, full of the desire to change the world, but without the desire to first change themselves.

Has Eric Learned the Inspector's Lesson?

In the final act, we have to ask ourselves if Eric has been transformed and will act on The Inspector's lesson.

He is much calmer here, taking on the role of an adult or even a parent, as he talks to his own parents, "I'm ashamed of you as well – yes both of you". We might interpret this as evidence of personal growth.

Eric becomes Priestley's proxy and spokesperson again. He accuses his father not just for his treatment of Eva, but of not being socialist, "You told us that a man has to make his own way, look after himself and mind his own business" and that the idea that "everybody has to look after everybody else" was an idea for "cranks".

This might give us the message that even flawed characters can change. It is very likely that most in Priestley audience in 1945 have committed acts about which they are now deeply ashamed – it is difficult to imagine living through 6 years of war and not committing shameful acts.

But Priestley also contrasts this with Eric's emotional state, again to undermine our faith in him. First, he is "shouting" and then in the next sentence, speaks "quietly, bitterly".

He keeps repeating "we all helped to kill her", so he accepts responsibility. But, does this just help him avoid full responsibility for all his own actions? He doesn't speak about his stealing the £50 from his father with any guilt. Nor does he admit to his full role in forcing himself on Eva.

However, his words now reveal that he does feel most guilty, without publicly admitting why. "You lot may be letting yourselves out nicely, but I can't. Nor can mother." We might look at these words as Priestley's proxy again, signalling who is most to blame. Priestley would therefore be accusing the corruption of the hypocritical patriarchy through Eric, and the damaging snobbery of social hierarchy and the class system through Sybil.

We'll come back to this view when we look at the part Gerald plays in Eva's tragedy.

Gerald Croft

Gerald in Act One

We have already seen that Gerald probably knows about Eric's affair with Eva. He also probably knows that Eric knows he, Gerald, has had an affair during the summer. Remember that he symbolises the patriarchy, coming as he does from landed gentry: his father is Sir Croft. Priestley makes this clear in Gerald's first line, when he refers to another of his father's titles as "the governor", deliberately linking him to government.

He also links Gerald immediately with "port" and "purple faced old men", implying that this is the kind of man Gerald will become. Finally, Gerald's first words also suggest he will choose to be hypocritical: "I don't pretend to know much about" port. This choice strongly hints that he does "pretend" about many other things, as we shall see.

Sheila's refusal to answer his questions at the family meal, and her complaint that he did not "come near" her all summer are all immediate clues that he has something to hide. Priestley primes us for his hypocrisy and his affair with Daisy.

He is also exceptionally vain, telling Sheila she can toast him, "drink to me". Priestley also uses this symbolically to show how women had to celebrate the patriarchy in 1912: their only route to influence or power is through marriage. This is why Sybil tells Sheila she must put up with Gerald's absences, "just as I had" with Birling. Priestley suggests that having affairs is simply what upper class men do, and even women advised each other to simply put up with it.

Priestley makes Mrs Birling comment on this again when Gerald presents Sheila with the engagement ring. She points out how "clever" Gerald is to present it "just at the right moment". In other words, the contract of marriage is a financial recompense for his infidelity. If we look back at her getting used to Birling's absences, she makes a point of saying that is only once they were "married". Priestley suggests that upper class women are therefore exploited as Eva is, the difference being that they are paid far more for it.

Priestley also makes Gerald agree with Birling when he declares that there will be "increasing prosperity" and that there is no need to worry about miners strikes and industrial unrest. On the one hand, he does this to show that Gerald is also just as wrong as Birling. On the other hand, the audience would see a further irony in this – for families like the Birlings and the Crofts, war was indeed very profitable. They had increased prosperity at a time when the rest of the country suffered.

Gerald is probably the cleverest character apart from The Inspector, and just as manipulative. As soon as The Inspector presses the doorbell, Gerald makes a joke at Eric's expense, suggesting that Eric has been "up to something". Although it is possible to see this only as Priestley being ironic, it may also be a signal from Gerald to Eric, that he knows Eric has been up to something with Eva. This is a form of blackmail, to prevent Eric from disclosing to Sheila what he knows about Gerald's affair.

Gerald Represents Capitalism

When Birling claims that Eva had to be sacked for leading a strike, Gerald immediately agrees that Birling "couldn't" have kept her on. There is no empathy in his view, he simply has to protect the profits of his business, even if it is unfair to the workforce. He even observes that workers would be "broke" because they had just had their holidays. He does not care that his business pays so little that a week off in some English seaside town would completely wipe out their savings for the year.

Gerald Confronts the Inspector from the Start

Gerald tells The Inspector that he is becoming "heavy handed", and points out "we're respectable citizens and not criminals". This is not the same as saying that they are not immoral, and not exploiting workers, just that what they are doing is not illegal.

Priestley wants to make the point that it should be illegal. Not paying workers enough to live on is morally the same as paying them enough, and then stealing from their wages. For this reason, The Inspector answers that "I wouldn't know where to draw the line" between "respectable citizens" and "criminals".

Gerald's reaction to this is significant. He doesn't disagree with it. He simply points out that he, the Birlings, and all the upper classes can get away with it: "Fortunately, it isn't left to you, is it?" "Fortunately" reveals how lucky he knows he is that capitalists can get away with this. The addition of "is it?" at the end of this statement also implies that Gerald believes he and other capitalists can keep getting away with it.

Gerald's Affair with Daisy Renton

Although Sheila is the first to expose Gerald's affair at the start, the language they both use strongly hints that she will forgive him after breaking off the engagement and that, after the end of the play, they will marry.

Gerald's first impulse is to lie, because Priestley wants to present all capitalists as hypocrites. He denies knowing any "Eva Smith". Sheila points out that she knows he is simply using his intelligence to maintain a veneer of honesty, as he knew her as "Daisy Renton". This is called sophistry – using clever arguments which appear true but which the speaker knows to be false.

Although Sheila insists on the truth, her language is also a kind of sophistry. She uses euphemism. Instead of asking for how long he had sex with Daisy, she only insists he "knew her very well". This is important, as while she is at her most angry now, her own language minimises what he has done. This will make it much easier for her to forgive him in the future. Clever as he is, Gerald picks up on this weakness in her resolve, calling her "darling" in order to manipulate her.

He immediately asks her to keep the affair secret from The Inspector. This might seem astonishingly arrogant. However, Priestley is again showing the corruption of the patriarchy. Gerald expects a woman to protect him even at the expense of her own happiness, in return for the financial security and status that marriage to him will offer her.

Gerald in Act Two

Gerald reveals his true motives here. He pretends (sophistry at work again) that he would rather protect Sheila against hearing "unpleasant and disturbing" things which she will "hate". However, he is really simply trying to protect himself.

When Sheila refuses to leave, he can only think in terms of a power relationship. Just as he has been playing a game of tit for tat with Eric, he now assumes that Sheila thinks in the same way: "now you want to see somebody else put through it." Sheila reacts as though Gerald thinks this is what she is like. However, it is much more revealing if we see it as simply what he is like. He imagines that everyone else is as manipulative as he is by instinct – it is merely that he believes he is better at it. Sheila calls it "selfish and vindictive". Gerald has certainly portrayed himself this way. Agreeing with Birling that Eva and the ringleaders should be sacked is "selfish" – it guarantees the business profits, and it is "vindictive" – it punishes the strikers with financial hardship and potential prostitution.

Gerald Tries to Deflect Blame

We see this immediately when The Inspector brings up Eric's drinking. A moment ago, he was pleading with Sheila not to reveal his affair with Daisy. However, as soon as it looks like Eric will be inspected, Gerald tells The Inspector, "he does drink pretty hard". He therefore tries to get The Inspector to focus on Eric. Remember, The Inspector did not seem to have arrived in order to question Gerald originally, and only chooses to speak to him when he realises he is going to marry Sheila. Gerald is holding on to this, and provoking The Inspector to forget about him, and deal with Eric.

Gerald's Account of the Affair is Implausible

Because Priestley has shown us that Gerald practises sophistry, and has a first instinct to lie, we are immediately distrustful of his explanation. When he says he "happened" to go into the Palace bar, we suspect his actual intention was to skip the show and go straight to the bar. When he explains that he went to the bar for "a drink" but that it is a "favourite haunt of women of the town" we suspect he was there precisely to look for one of these "women".

When he claims he hates "those hard-eyed dough-faced women" we suspect he has gone looking for someone newer to prostitution, someone younger. He immediately juxtaposes this with how he "noticed" Eva. He focuses on her being "pretty" with "soft brown hair and big dark eyes". Priestley wants us to realise how she has become a thing of value to powerful men because of her looks. But he also wants Eric and the others to hear the same description, because this makes it much more likely that they are dealing with the same girl, and it makes Gerald's later denial of this yet another example of sophistry.

The Semantic Field of Death

The most perceptive readers will have noticed Gerald's use of the word "haunt" in a play featuring a probably supernatural "Goole". This reminder of death is echoed by his description of Alderman Meggarty, who has cornered Eva, "with that obscene fat carcass of his". Symbolically, at the moment she meets Gerald, she is already in the presence of death.

Another level of symbolism here is that Gerald objects to what is happening to Eva not because she is being pressed for sex, but because Meggarty is not the dominant, desirable male, being "old" and "fat". This is what makes him "obscene" in Gerald's eyes, not that he wants to have sex with vulnerable, attractive women.

Gerald is immediately attracted to her, "she looked young and fresh and charming". Notice that he does not speak about her beauty. What attracts him are the things he can take from her, her youth and innocence. These are also the qualities which will make her easier to exploit. And what does he mean by "charming", when he notices her "wedged" in the corner by Meggarty? He can only mean that she does not fight back, that she is compliant, and doesn't want to cause a scene. In other words, she probably won't turn down the much younger and more handsome Gerald.

You will also remember that a plucked flower will die, and Eva has symbolically associated herself with death, choosing the name Daisy.

Gerald's Capitalist Exploitation of Daisy for Sex

Right at the start Gerald doesn't offer to help her. He presents leaving with him as an exchange: "told the girl that if she didn't want any more of that sort of thing, she'd better let me take her out of there."

Notice how he does not use her name here, she is just "the girl". He doesn't care about her as an individual person, she is simply a vulnerable young girl who is far more likely to give him sex. Notice how he phrases what she might "want" and juxtaposes it with what she should "let me take". Although he is not directly asking her to have sex with him, his choice of words reveal that is the exchange he has in mind.

We notice that, rather than buy her food, he first gets her to drink "one or two". When he finds out she is hungry, he "made" the hotel staff get her some food, which implies how terribly late it must be. It also suggests there has been time to get her more than a little drunk, drinking on an empty stomach.

When he describes her poverty, he uses the phrase "desperately hard up". We notice his focus on her desperation. She is in no position to refuse his advances, because the alternative is straight forward prostitution at the Palace bar.

The Inspector points us to this straight away. As soon as Gerald tells us that she was desperate, The Inspector states: "then you decided to keep her – as your mistress?"

Gerald's Sophistry About Having Daisy as a Mistress

The use of the word "keep" here also subtly suggests she is a possession. A "mistress" is socially much superior to a prostitute, and she is much more protected against violence and sexually transmitted disease. In this way, Gerald can convince himself that he is doing her a favour, rather than exploiting her for sex.

We now find out that Gerald has probably been planning this for some time. He hides this fact by not beginning chronologically with this element of his story:

"It happened that a friend of mine … had gone off to Canada for six months and had let me have the key of a nice little set of rooms"

Again, we notice that passive use of "happened", pretending that his friend did not give him the keys to this flat precisely so he could set up a mistress there. He also wastes no time – he has the affair over "spring and summer" and March to August is exactly "six months" – this encounter didn't just happen, Gerald made it happen immediately, just as soon as he got the "nice little set of rooms".

Gerald Rents Daisy Cheaply

Again, his language reveals how she is a possession. He says he "installed her" there like an object. He asks The Inspector and Sheila to believe "I didn't install her there so that I could make love to her" which is ironically true, he simply wanted to have sex with her, and no "love" was involved on his part.

He practises sophistry again when he says, "I didn't ask for anything in return" for the "money" he "made her" take, and for the lodgings. We know this simply means he didn't have to spell out the terms of the exchange – they both knew she was expected to have sex with him.

To make clear how little love was involved, and how he always saw her as a disposable possession, he tells Sheila that he "adored" being her "fairy prince" only "for a time". Once her freshness had worn off, he was ready to move on to another novelty – in this case, engagement to Sheila.

Worse than this, he can't even be bothered to pretend to Daisy that he hasn't grown tired of her, so "Daisy knew it was coming to an end". Although he claims the end was brought about by needing to go away for business for a few weeks, we know the real reason is that his friend was returning from Canada.

This would mean that Gerald would have to pay for a flat to put her in. This would cost far more than the little he had paid her, "she'd lived very economically on what I'd allowed her". In six months she had managed to save hardly any, because he pays her off with a "parting gift" which, together with her savings, only allows her to book a room at the seaside for two months in the autumn, when tourists have left, and accommodation is cheaper.

Priestley wants us to see the relationship in these financial terms, because he is making the point that all relationships in the patriarchy are structured financially this way, and therefore powerful men will always exploit less powerful women. He laces this with irony, because Daisy tells Gerald "she'd been happier than she'd ever been before". In other words, the lives of women are so powerless, that even this level of exploitation is better than working in a factory for subsistence wages.

Gerald Plans to Expose the Inspector

Gerald asks for permission to leave. He claims, "as I'm rather more – upset – by this business than I probably appear to be – and – well, I'd like to be alone for a while – …"

Again, we should notice his choice of language. He can't fake the required level of distress at learning that his mistress has committed suicide, and he is worried that Sheila and The Inspector will have noticed this. So he claims that he will "probably appear" not to be as upset as he is. In fact, this is a lie. We know this from the way he has treated Daisy already. But we will also learn it in Act 3, when we discover he has gone out looking for a policeman, to find out if Inspector Goole is a "fraud", not because he cares about Daisy's death.

His language also reveals his true thoughts when he calls Eva's suicide and their affair "this business". This euphemism reveals his unconscious thought – his relationship with Daisy was purely "business", and he paid her for what he wanted until he wanted her no more.

Does Gerald Deceive Sheila Even When he Confesses?

Sheila's reaction suggests that she spots none of this in Gerald, and simply accepts his story, with himself as the "hero", "the fairy prince" who has tried to "help … out of pity" rather than exploit out of lust.

She gives back the engagement ring, but is already starting to forgive him, and gives him permission to come back, telling him they will "have to start all over again".

This is a greater tragedy perhaps. When Priestley plants this seed of forgiveness, he is not suggesting that Gerald has learned The Inspector's lesson. His corrupt sexual exploitation is just glossed over as "pity" and "help", a kindness.

Priestley is subtly pointing out that in a patriarchy, women are so conditioned to being powerless and under the control of men, that they are also conditioned to think the best of them, even when faced with evidence of their worst behaviour. Although Sheila is not self-aware enough to spot this, in 1945 the patriarchy has been violently disrupted by war. Priestley believes that the young women in his audience will see Sheila's mistake, and understand Gerald for what he is, a symbol of oppression.

Gerald in Act Three

Gerald Pretends it is Not the Same Girl

Gerald claims to have simply bumped in to a policeman. "I met a police sergeant I know down the road". Priestley drops clues as to how implausible this is. He would be much more likely to meet a police constable, a bobby on the beat. A "sergeant" would be at a police station, not "down the road". Moreover, how would Gerald get to "know" a police sergeant? This suggests a link over time, in which Gerald has already had dealings with the police. It also suggests he has deliberately gone looking for this sergeant, suspicious that The Inspector is not real.

Having exposed The Inspector as "a hoax" he now asks, "how do we know it's the same girl?" We know, from Eva's timeline, and from the details Gerald himself remembers, she is incredibly likely to be the same girl. Let's review what he told The Inspector in Act 2:

1. "she'd lost both parents...
2. she came originally from somewhere outside Brumley...
3. she'd had a job in one of the works here...
4. and had had to leave after a strike.
5. She said something about the shop too"

Then, add to that the physical description, her age and the exact matches in the timeline and it becomes highly implausible that this is not the same girl. Priestley draws our attention to this because so much of the corroborating evidence comes from Gerald himself. In other words, he knows it must be the same girl with more certainty than any of the other characters. And yet, he is the person most keen to prove she is not. This is his sophistry at work again.

Priestley probably does this to attack the ruling classes of 1945. Who will be in power then? Gerald, and the men he represents. Possibly too old to have joined the front line in 1914, he is much more likely to be one of the survivors who would take control of industry and power between the wars. It is men like him who will be running the country, standing as Conservative MPs. Priestley wants his audience to see this hypocrisy for themselves.

His focus on "the photograph" is therefore a ploy to avoid responsibility. If he can convince himself and the Birlings that they were all different "girls", then it will be easier for them to maintain a fiction that what they did to these girls didn't matter so much. Similarly, if none of the women killed themselves, he seems to suggest, he and the Birlings are absolved from guilt at how they have exploited someone.

Even the Birling's see this for what it is. They know the truth of what they have done, but want to hide behind whether there is "proof". We can see this in the way Mrs Birling congratulates Gerald for his sophistry:

"And I must say, Gerald, you've argued this very cleverly, and I'm most grateful."

She is not proud of him for uncovering the truth. She is "grateful" that he has provided a convenient lie. There is no actual proof it was the same girl, so there is no actual proof they did anything wrong. That she sees this as an argument which he has constructed "cleverly" reinforces that she knows it is a convenient fiction.

Gerald Summons the Second Inspector
It appears to be Birling's words which summon The Inspector. They are again cut short by the telephone announcing that an inspector is coming: "And they can't even take a joke." So, we might say that Priestley stages this at the moment when the older generation refuse to learn The Inspector's lesson.

But there is another way of looking at this ending. Directly preceding Birling's line are these:

> "Gerald: Everything's all right now, Sheila. (Holds up the ring.) What about this ring?
>
> Sheila: No, not yet. It's too soon. I must think."

We can see this as proof that none of them will live by The Inspector's lesson. When Gerald asks her to take back "the ring", the telephone will echo his words "this ring". He even instructs Gerald to show it to us "Holds up the ring." Priestley could simply have made Gerald ask, "What about our engagement?" He wants us to associate this question with the ringing of the phone.

The other factor is Sheila's reaction: "not yet" certainly implies her future answer will be to accept and marry Gerald.

Looked at in this way, The Inspector is summoned again because they have *all* turned away from his lesson, even Sheila.

Sheila Birling

Sheila in Act One

There are three themes affecting Sheila in the play.

1. Her connection to The Inspector and the supernatural
2. Her role in providing a feminist perspective
3. Her promotion of The Inspector's socialist message

1945 is a very early moment in history for Priestley to be taking a feminist perspective. However, it is women voters who are going to make the difference in electing a Labour government and rejecting the capitalist society they have grown up in. To encourage this, Priestley constructs Sheila so that we can understand why even she, a rich, privileged, upper class woman, would wish to reject the capitalist upbringing she has had.

In terms of the morality play, Sheila's sin of vanity is no worse than any of the other 'deadly sins'. However, when looked at through the lens of socialism, Sheila's sin is probably worse than any of the other characters. This is not the conventional view, which sees Sheila as the least guilty character.

In a socialist society, everyone receives a fair wage for their work. This is most true for Eva when she works at Milwards. Although Birling had her sacked from his factory, her job there would have been noisy, repetitive, difficult and hazardous. In contrast, Milwards is clearly a high-class store, with a far better working environment and one which will be far more sociable. Losing this job is far more of a loss than at Birling's factory – we can guess that there might only be 100 such jobs at Milwards, but there would probably be over 1000 working at each of Birlings and Crofts.

We can confidently say that losing the Milwards job was far worse for Eva than being sacked by Birling. Without this sacking, Eva would never have had to consider prostitution.

How does Priestley Make us Sympathetic to Sheila?
The first thing Priestley does with Sheila is introduce us to a moment of doubt, where we can see that all is not well in her relationship with Gerald. The stage directions reveal that Sheila is caught in two minds, "half serious, half playful". She is "serious" because she suspects Gerald has been unfaithful. She is "playful" because she still sees it as her role to put up with this, and act flirtatiously in order to be a good prospect for marriage.

This is the heart of the feminist conflict. In a patriarchal society, Sheila is completely dependent on men. The best life she can create for herself is to marry as well as she can – she needs someone loving, handsome, wealthy and well placed in the social hierarchy. With no way of earning her own income, which of these items on her list is most important, and which is most easy to compromise?

Priestley uses this dilemma to create conflict in Sheila's mind. At the very moment that Gerald is going to bring out the engagement ring, Sheila brings up the events of "last summer". Now this is quite a brave thing to do because Gerald might choose to break the engagement off, fearful that his guilty secret will come out. When he talks about being "busy" with "business" she pushes the point: "yes, that's what you say." It's letting him know that she suspects him, but she is not demanding that he tells the truth. Sheila here is her mother's daughter, speaking in code. She raises this at a family meal, as though to warn Gerald that he can't afford for his affairs to become public knowledge.

Will Sheila Allow Gerald to Have Affairs?
Her mother has clearly trained her to accept this: "when you're married you realise that men with important work to do sometimes have to spend nearly all their time and energy on their business." However, Priestley also escalates the conflict here. If we focus on "married" we can see this as a more dramatic warning from Sybil to her daughter. Once Sheila is "married" to Gerald, his behaviour is likely to be even worse, with more periods away from her. From a feminist perspective, Priestley is showing that Gerald only has a motive to behave well towards Sheila while he is wooing her, as she can always refuse his offer of engagement. Once married, however, she may have too much to lose, and he won't have to work so hard to ensure her happiness.

You might argue that Mrs Birling is only talking about "business", not her husband's affairs. However, the phrase "just as I did" strongly suggests that it is not work that took Birling away, but affairs. If it were work, she would say 'just as I have'. After all, Birling's work has only grown more successful, and he would have a greater need to travel now than he did earlier in their marriage. Instead, his absences are far less, because he is older, and much less inclined to have affairs now.

Sheila decides to risk calling Gerald's bluff: "you be careful." One way of reading this is as a warning not to take her for granted with further absences once they are married. A more cynical interpretation is that she is only warning him to be discrete, to be "careful" that Sheila does not find out about his affairs.

How Likely is it that Sheila Knows Gerald has had an Affair or Affairs?
Eric's reaction to Gerald saying "Oh – I will" be careful, is a sudden "guffaw". Now many readers take this to simply signify that Eric is drunk. He is clearly suggesting that there is very little chance that Gerald is going to be "careful". This further suggests that Gerald hasn't just had a single affair. He is maybe well known for it, for Eric to find out about it, and to be so dismissive of the possibility of Gerald being "careful". This strongly suggests that Sheila also knows he is having affairs, that this is simply a pattern of behaviour he won't break. We can see her warning then as the need to be discrete, rather than an expectation that he will stop.

So, Sheila is clearly struggling with the morality of the time, this accepted idea that women would simply have to put up with their rich and powerful husbands having affairs when they wanted. The emancipated women of 1945 would see Sheila's dilemma, and also recognise that they would not have to make the same compromise.

However, for upper class women, the problem would in fact be the same. Even more importantly, the pressures after 1918, with nearly one million British men killed, would have meant there was far more pressure on women to accept their husbands having affairs. Put simply, there were far more women than men, and they could dictate more of their own terms. There were over 380,000 military deaths of UK combatants in The Second World War, and women would again feel this conflict between marrying for love, or for economic security.

Sheila's Marriage is a Business
Priestley dramatises the conflict further by presenting it in capitalist terms. He makes Birling describe Sheila's marriage as a business alliance, where "Crofts and Birlings are no longer competing but are working together". Sybil objects to this in a telling way. She doesn't tell Birling that he is wrong to view the marriage in capitalist terms. Instead, she advises him, "I don't think you ought to talk business on an occasion like this." Here she simply means it is too unromantic to mention the truth at their engagement – it should remain unspoken because it is unromantic, not because it is untrue.

Sheila's reply is unusually incoherent, "All wrong." This is a sentence without a verb, not a proper sentence. It is as though she can't find the words to express what is wrong with Birling's view. This is again because, intellectually, she knows it is true. Her marriage is simply making the best economic match that she can. This only happens because the patriarchal society forces her to make this compromise.

Sheila is her Father's Property
Both a feminist and socialist perspective will see Sheila as a possession of her father. She could find her own way in life up to a point. She has not been to university, unlike Eric. She will only have been educated in ways which make her attractive to upper class men. She'll have learned to manage a housekeeper, a cook, a maid or two, but she won't have been prepared in any way for marrying someone socially inferior, without serving staff. Although she could do it, it is totally outside her experience.

It is even more difficult for her to imagine this other life because of the way Birling treats her. He describes her in front of Gerald, "She'll make you happy" as though that is what she has been brought up to do.

When Birling describes the marriage, he says "Sheila's a lucky girl – and I think you're a pretty fortunate young man too, Gerald." He clearly sees Sheila as luckier than Gerald. She should therefore be more grateful at the marriage than Gerald is. If he were talking about love, then he wouldn't describe Gerald as being "pretty fortunate", he would say Gerald was very fortunate, because Sheila has so much love for him. However, he is thinking in purely financial terms, so yes, Sheila is "lucky" because Crofts is bigger than Birling is, but Gerald is also lucky because there is going to be an alliance with a large, though not as large, company. That's why he is only "pretty fortunate".

This puts Sheila in a really difficult position. She clearly appears to love Gerald, and she also realises that it is somehow her family duty as a daughter to go along with this match, because it's such a fortunate one for the fortunes of the family.

However, when she proposes a toast, she decides that actually she should focus just on Gerald. And she wants to emphasise her personal connection and love for him: "I drink to you Gerald."

The conversation between them next feels slightly ominous. Instead of saying he's going to make her as happy as she deserves to be, he says "I hope I can make you as happy as you deserve to be," already introducing doubt, perhaps self-doubt. Perhaps he does not believe he can remain faithful to her or even to keep his affairs a secret.

Again she has to hide her true feelings. One way of reading this is that she sees Gerald's words as a real mark of love, to make her happy, and that's why she warns, "I'll start weeping". Alternatively, we can see an underlying tension here. Sheila might realise that he knows he can't be faithful to her, and the "weeping" then becomes an acknowledgement that he is offering a weak kind of love.

Sheila Can't Escape Capitalism and the Social Hierarchy
Priestley presents Sheila at her most childish when she receives the engagement ring, calling her parents "mummy" and "daddy". Priestley does this because he makes her most fixated on wealth at this stage: he implies that the love of wealth is a childish desire we should resist as we become adult. In other words, capitalism is a childish wish; socialism is the mark of adult understanding.

She asks, "Is it the one you wanted me to have?" perhaps suggesting that it was expensive – her question is then asking if he could afford it. Her excitement therefore isn't about being engaged, it's about receiving this particular, expensive ring. We can also see that she treats it as more important than Gerald, who she kisses "hastily". We then watch her on stage, putting on the ring "admiringly", and she expresses more love for it than she has for Gerald: "I'll never let it go out of my sight for an instant." Indeed, she might be making a point that, while Gerald will no doubt leave her frequently for "business", the ring can be relied on to be utterly faithful, unlike Gerald who is often "out of my sight". The ring is also a symbol of her financial security.

Her mother also takes the same view. Gerald himself is not important, it is what the ring symbolises which matters. This is why she immediately tries to take Sheila away, "I think Sheila and I had better go into the drawing room." In this world, celebrating her new financial security, together as women, is far more important than Sheila showering Gerald with any affection.

It's also revealing that Sheila calls the ring "a beauty". Eva's "Beauty" will be Sheila's motive for having her sacked. This illustrates, from a feminist perspective, how upper-class women in particular are forced to pay for too much attention to their looks because that is the way they are going to attract a wealthy husband. This patriarchal society equates female beauty with wealth. Priestley takes that to its logical next step, when Eva can only exploit the financial value of her beauty through sex in exchange for financial security, however temporary.

Priestley makes this point more strongly when Sheila first hears of Eva's death, which is why he makes her ask, was Eva "Pretty?" This is the primary way in which society has taught women to judge each other.

Sheila again picks up on Priestley's feminist message when she attacks her father's capitalist reasons for sacking Eva: "But these girls aren't cheap labour – they're people." She is not simply protesting about capitalism, where workers are exploited by the rich, she's picking on the fact that these women, or "girls", so less than adults, and are now treated as less than people: "cheap labour". And she emphasises that neither of these is correct: "They're people", not to be diminished as childlike and "girls", and not to be diminished as a thing, "labour", something that can be bought and sold.

This is exactly The Inspector's message which Sheila has already learned: "sometimes if we tried to put ourselves in the place of these young women." Notice that he picks up on Sheila's objection to them as "girls" and calls them "women", because he is carrying Priestley's feminist message also. We might expect Sheila to simply go along with this.

The Patriarchal Society Corrupts all Women
Next Priestley returns to the feminist perspective, marrying it with the morality play, so we discover Sheila's vanity. So as soon as Sheila hears that Eva was fired after a customer complaint, she asks "What did this girl look like?" This is a surprise. The incident happened a nearly two years ago, and Eva was only in the post a couple of months. So, Sheila may only have seen her once. The only reason that she has remembered the Eva's looks is because she was so attractive.

Here Priestley is suggesting that this patriarchal society has corrupted women – it makes all women vain, because it is the only way they can maintain their value in a society which places so much worth on appearance. For young, rich women like Sheila, the hierarchy isn't just about wealth, they must be attractive to maintain that wealth through marriage. This is why Sheila turns on Eva, because Eva is more attractive than her. We can also look at this in simple capitalist terms. Eva is an economic threat to Sheila, because she is more attractive than Sheila. Readers might think this is a step too far, but consider this – Eva does replace Sheila in Gerald's affections, even if only for a few months. She is also able to marry Eric, as he proposes to her. It is her decision not to accept this proposal.

Sheila is the Most Honest Character
Priestley decides to make Sheila unique amongst all the other characters, because she is the only one who attempts to be honest. Her father first claims he can't remember who Eva Smith was. Her mother will do the same. Gerald denied that he had had an affair with Daisy Renton, then pretended that he had simply wanted to "help" her, rather than taking on his friend's lodging for the express purpose of installing a mistress. Mrs Birling likewise denies having done anything wrong and also initially having met Eva. Eric appears to be honest, but crucially says he can't remember what happened that night he forced himself into Eva's flat, leaving it open for us to assume that he has probably raped her. But this is not something he will admit, even to himself.

In contrast, Sheila admits that she persuaded, or was going to persuade her mother to close their "account" and that she had "been in a bad temper". She therefore admits she did not have a proper reason for getting Eva sacked. But, as she says, "at least, I'm trying to tell the truth." This allows us to think, if any character can change, it's going to be Sheila.

She uses this honesty to ask Gerald to admit to his affairs, "I expect you've done things you're ashamed of too." Notice the plural. Because he is an upper-class man, Sheila does not imagine just a single thing he has done which is shameful. If he has had an affair, she probably thinks this is only one in a pattern of behaviour.

Gerald is incredibly reluctant to reveal his affair in front of Sheila, asking if they can "leave it at that". However, Sheila's questioning almost suggests that she will be relieved if he has only had the one affair: "Were you seeing her last spring and summer"? If we emphasise "and" it could show her expectation that he would have had affairs with different women, changing them as often as the seasons. Similarly, if we emphasise "her" we can see her checking that there is only one "girl".

Priestley Focuses on Eva and Sheila Because he has a Feminist Message

From a feminist perspective, Priestley would be highlighting the awful compromise women have to make in their marriages, in order to achieve financial independence. It's interesting that, in recalling the incident where she got Eva sacked, Sheila uses the very language that her mother uses several times later in the play: "this girl had been very impertinent".

Impertinence means rudeness towards people entitled to (or who believe they are entitled to) respect. Sheila clearly felt at this point that she was entitled to respect, as a wealthy woman. However, perhaps what makes her so vindictive, is that she is not wealthy in her own right. Her power is only borrowed from the fact that her mother is a customer, and from the fact that her father is "well known in the town" as an influential man.

If she, Eva, had "been some miserable plain little creature, I don't suppose I'd have done it." So, looking at the play as a morality play, we can see that Eva has been treated so poorly because of Sheila's vanity. However, from a feminist perspective, we see that that vanity is only so important because it's the only way that Sheila can make herself marketable to attractive, rich men. This is what she means by "looked as if she could take care of herself."

Priestley emphasises the theme of the morality play when The Inspector points out that her sin is actually envy: she is "jealous of" Eva's looks. However, he links the morality play, not to Christianity, but to capitalism and feminism: "so you used the power you had as a daughter of a good customer and also of a man well known in the town, to punish the girl". This "power" is clearly linked to the financial, capitalist power of her parents here. However, notice how The Inspector places the most important power relationship first, her power only comes "as a daughter". Priestley is highlighting that society gives her no real power as a woman; she is totally subservient to her parents. So, it is no surprise that Sheila mirrors this relationship, making Eva totally subservient to her.

From the feminist perspective, Priestley is asking us as an audience just how many mistresses Gerald could have before we would review Sheila's marriage to Gerald as being completely unacceptable.

Gerald simply wants to keep the affair secret from The Inspector. This changes Sheila's behaviour. She becomes hysterical, which will happen quite a few times in the play. Priestley might do this to show that The Inspector is having such a profound effect on her. But, another way of looking at it is to think that it first happened here. What seems to have had this profound effect is realising that she has to marry someone who is deeply unfaithful.

The Inspector is Priestley's Proxy. Sheila is The Inspector's Proxy.
Priestley ends Act 1 with Sheila having replaced The Inspector, who is off stage. Priestley wants us to see her growing link to The Inspector. She warns Gerald, "We haven't much time", which The Inspector will repeat later in the play.

She also begins to sense the future more clearly, "And I hate to think how much he knows that we don't know yet. You'll see. You'll see." This repetition emphasises Priestley's message, that they must all "see" what they have done, and learn from it. However, even in this act, Priestley suggests that they probably won't. He undermines her with the stage direction, *"laughs rather hysterically"*, so that we don't trust her judgement or, if we do, we don't trust her ability to be rational once she has learned The Inspector's lesson.

<u>Sheila in Act Two</u>

Sheila Senses the Inspector's Supernatural Power
The second act also begins with Sheila "getting hysterical now". The Inspector is actually keen for her to go, telling her "I don't want to keep you here". However, Priestley uses her as a catalyst to get the other characters, as The Inspector puts it, "to share our guilt."

This is important, as it is the act of sharing which will lead to joint action and forgiveness. This will resonate with a theatre audience, which has a shared experience of the action and characters on stage, and the "our" also invites the audience to share in this guilt. After all, many of them will come from Sheila and Gerald's generation, as well as their parents, and Priestley is also accusing them of not making sufficient difference to society between the wars, by 1945.

Sheila also becomes increasingly connected to The Inspector in this act, and perhaps begins to realise he is not a real inspector, but a supernatural presence. Priestley hints at this in his stage directions, *"she stares at him wonderingly and dubiously".* She is both impressed at him, and suspicious, as "dubiously" indicates.

Priestley also makes The Inspector allude to this when Sheila tries to warn her mother not to begin so "confidently" rejecting The Inspector's enquiries. He observes that he has made an "impression" on Sheila, "we often do on the young ones. They're more impressionable." So, we are invited to believe that Sheila has begun to see the family, and the capitalist society, through The Inspector's socialist eyes.

Now Sheila begins to speak as though she is repeating a lesson, *"slowly, carefully now"* and warns her mother, "you mustn't try to build up a kind of wall between us and that girl." This wall is a metaphor for her mother's snobbery, and the divisions caused by social class.

Sheila Becomes the Inspector's Proxy, Seeking the Truth
Priestley also wants us to see how much she has changed when she begins laughing at her mother's use of "impertinent", which Sheila herself used only minutes before, but which she now rejects, "because impertinent is such a silly word."

Sheila now sees the class system and snobbery as a "pretence". It is even more dangerous, because it becomes a habit, so that the Birlings, and the ruling classes as a whole, develop the habit of pretending in all aspects of their lives. This is why she reveals Eric's alcoholism, "He's been steadily drinking too much for the last two years." This revelation also reveals how deliberately blind Mrs Birling has become. A feminist perspective might argue that this is just what a patriarchal society does to its women – the only way for a woman to believe she has influence and power is to pretend to do so. Here we see she does not even have the power to look after her son.

So, Sheila is now just as keen to expose the rest of the family as The Inspector is, so that they will learn his lesson: "and probably between us we killed her."

Ultimately Sheila is Corrupted by the Patriarchy, Afraid of the Truth

However, Priestley presents us with a problem with her parting words to Gerald. Has she really learned The Inspector's lesson? As we saw in the section on Gerald, he repeatedly lies about his intentions with Daisy. Yet Sheila appears to accept them at face value: "And now at least you've been honest. And I believe what you told us about the way you helped her at first. Just out of pity." As an audience, we find it very difficult to agree with her assessment of Gerald's motives. That final curtailed sentence also suggests that she herself does not really believe it is his real motive.

We might also be disturbed by how she appears to blame herself for Gerald's affair, "And it was my fault really that she was so desperate when you first met her." The addition of the word "really" is an afterthought. If she truly believed this, it would be phrased "and it really was my fault". We are left with the worrying question as to whether she is lying to Gerald, or also lying to herself. If the latter, she is very much like her mother, only a younger and less self-deceiving version.

Priestley answers the question partly with her next invitation to Gerald, "We'd have to start all over again". Therefore, returning the engagement ring is not an act of finality, it is merely the beginning of negotiations to say that she will have him back.

We might have no moral issue with this in a play with such Christian themes. We would be happy for her to forgive, so long as Gerald's repentance is real. But, as we shall see in the Act Three, and as Gerald has already demonstrated here, he does not feel much guilt at all.

Sheila ends the act by being the first character to realise that Mrs Birling is implicating her own son as being "the chief culprit" and "he ought to be dealt with very severely". Her reaction, however, highlights her powerlessness, and she can only weep, "Sheila *begins crying quietly*". This is a deliberate contrast to how she ended Act One, staring at Gerald "triumphantly".

Sheila in Act Three

Sheila is Powerless

At the beginning of Act Three, Priestley removes Sheila and Mrs Birling from the stage, which is very odd because they return within about 400 words. Perhaps this is because Birling suspects that Eric will reveal details of his rape of Eva. In fact he doesn't, and Sheila returns, led by her mother, exclaiming that bringing Sybil back "isn't my fault." Perhaps Priestley does this to suggest that Sheila, as part of the younger generation, will not be able to overcome the influence of her parents, even after the end of the play when she feels she has learned The Inspector's lesson.

Indeed, when Eric becomes threatening to his mother, Sheila stands by her, "(*frightened*) Eric, don't – don't". She jumps in even before Birling does, which strongly suggests Mrs Birling still has a powerful influence over her, much more than her bond with Eric. It is easy to forget this when the act ends with Sheila and Eric in apparent agreement about The Inspector's lesson.

Sheila also fails to take any initiative once The Inspector leaves. Instead, Priestley makes sure she is seen as largely powerless, "*Sheila is still quietly crying.*" To reveal her powerlessness more clearly, Priestley also makes sure that only one character seems to have any power to act, "*Birling, the only active one.*" It isn't a coincidence that the only character who feels able to act independently is head of the household and, symbolically, head of the patriarchy. Here Priestley suggests that Birling will remain in control and the "famous younger generation" will remain without power.

Sheila Becomes a Teacher

Sheila now takes on the role of a teacher, trying to get her parents to learn The Inspector's lesson, "The point is, you don't seem to have learnt anything." Sheila also teaches us about The Inspector's supernatural origins. She is the first to point out that he is "not" a "police inspector". She also describes him as having "something curious about him" which hints at the supernatural. Next, she confirms her suspicions with a reference to his having some sort of supernatural knowledge, "We hardly ever told him anything he didn't know."

Sheila Remains Loyal to her Family

However, although she tells her family that it does not matter if The Inspector was a "hoax" and that "he made us confess", she still stays loyal to her parents. This is why, when Gerald returns, she doesn't choose to tell him about what Eric and Mrs Birling did to Eva, "You see, Gerald, you haven't to know the rest of our crimes and idiocies." Her tone reveals that she wants to tell him, but her actions remain loyal. This is also another hint that she is protecting her investment in Gerald – if he discovers that Eric is probably a rapist, and is definitely a thief, he is much less likely to want to marry her.

In fact, Eric reveals being a thief to Gerald, when he accuses his parents of not learning The Inspector's lesson, "It's what happened to the girl and what we all did to her that matters." Sheila immediately agrees, "You're just beginning to pretend all over again." Although she is insisting that they learn The Inspector's lesson, she has stopped taking the initiative. Instead, the struggle for centre stage is taken up by Eric and Gerald. Priestley does this again to show where true power lies, with the males. They take over the debate about The Inspector and Priestley makes sure that Sheila, as a woman, has to take a back seat.

Sheila is Silenced by the Patriarchal Society of 1912
Some readers assume this is an example of Priestley's sexism, that being part of the patriarchal society, he is not even aware of it. However, when we consider how Priestley has chosen a female victim, in Eva, and has decided that Sheila alone will understand The Inspector's supernatural powers, we can clearly see this is unlikely. Instead, Priestley wants to show his audience that we should be on Sheila's side.

If Sheila fails to live out The Inspector's lesson, it isn't because she hasn't learned it. It is because the patriarchal, capitalist society of her time, 1912, did not let her. However now, Priestley seems to be saying, now in 1945, women really can have an equal voice to men.

Even Though Sheila is Arguably the Most Important Character, She Probably Fails
For this reason, Priestley gives Sheila most of the final lines of the play. Priestley sets this up as a conflict between Sheila and her father. Of the final 364 words of dialogue, 157 are given to Birling, and 170 to Sheila.

To emphasise her importance, Priestley also makes sure that she carries The Inspector's message (which of course is a proxy for Priestley's message):

"No, because I remember what he said, how he looked, and what he made me feel. Fire and blood and anguish."

However, Priestley does not allow these to be her final words. Instead he introduces the idea that she won't be able to stick to her resolve and learn that lesson. Instead, "fire and blood and anguish" come in the form of both world wars. Priestley is making clear that, despite her intentions, learning the lesson was not enough. Sheila, like all the young women of 1912, simply doesn't have enough power or influence to change society.

For an upper-class woman like Sheila the only way to have any kind of equality with her parents is to marry. Consequently, Priestley hints with her final words that she will marry Gerald. He offers her the ring, and she cannot simply refuse, but hints at future acceptance: "No, not yet. It's too soon. I must think."

<u>**Sybil Birling**</u>

Mrs Birling in Act One

She Represents the Cruel Control of the Class System
Sybil Birling's first impression on the audience is that she needs to be in control. This is why Birling has to encourage her to have a drink, "you must take a little tonight." This exchange also asks us to question the power relationship in the family, which Priestley's audience would also pick up on, as she is seated at the opposite end of the table to her husband, again symbolising how she wants control of the family.

Although she agrees to have a little drink, she immediately delivers instructions to Edna. These are irrelevant in themselves, and just serve to remind everyone that she is the dominant figure in the household.

This need may be because managing the household is the main way an upper-class woman can assert her authority in this patriarchal society. Alternatively, when we refer back to the opening stage directions, we realise that she has chosen to be "cold", and Priestley does not wish us to be too sympathetic to her controlling personality.

We see how mean spirited she is when she tells off her husband "reproachfully" for asking her to congratulate "cook" for the quality of dinner. Her reason, "you're not supposed to say such things" reveals her obsession with social class.

Priestley uses her unpleasant personality to suggest that the class system encourages the upper classes to deny basic good manners, and treat everyone else as inferior. He wants us to dislike her immediately and, through her, dislike the social hierarchy she represents.

Sybil is Wilfully Blind to Reality
As we've seen, she is keen for Sheila to put up with Gerald's infidelity, "just as I had". Being betrayed by men is a part of the social hierarchy, and the price an upper-class woman must pay for marrying a rich or upper-class man. Priestley uses this to attack the patriarchy, but also to attack her for not insisting on higher standards for her daughter.

At the heart of her snobbery we can see a kind of deliberate blindness. We see this most clearly in her obsession with language, with word choice. By focusing on word choice she is able to ignore the thing being described. For example, she tells Sheila to put up with Gerald being away on "business", which we understand is a euphemism for having a mistress. She tells Arthur not to "say such things" which means he cannot show common courtesy or kindness. She objects to Sheila using the word "squiffy" about Eric, "what an expression", so she can ignore the fact that Eric is an alcoholic.

She also tells Birling off again, "Now, Arthur, I don't think you ought to talk business on an occasion like this." Priestley does this ironically, so that it appears she is telling him off for treating Sheila's engagement as a "business" arrangement. However, by the end of the sentence we realise she simply means that it is wrong to mention it, "on an occasion like this" which is supposed to be romantic. She is very happy to, symbolically, sell Sheila off to the highest bidder. In this way, it really is a "business" arrangement.

Once the engagement ring has been exchanged, Sybil is keen for the "men" to talk about business, and she tries to take Sheila away. Because Birling insists on making a long speech, she has ample opportunity to watch Eric. When Birling has finished, she decides to remove Eric, "Eric – I want you a minute." What has made her change her mind? It is very likely that she has noticed his drunken behaviour. By dealing with this off stage, Priestley again symbolises how the upper classes try to hide their failings from others, so that they can still pretend they are superior. However, when Mrs Birling later denies that Eric drinks too much, we are ready to believe that she is lying. Her need for superiority is so powerful that she is even able to lie convincingly to herself.

Mrs Birling is Worse than Birling

Priestley keeps her off stage while we discover details of how Birling sacked Eva, and also that Sheila had her sacked from Milwards. When Sheila is upset at what she's done, she leaves the stage crying. Interestingly, she returns saying, "I've told my father – he didn't seem to think it amounted to much." Priestley wants to make clear that however horrible Birling has appeared to be, his wife appears so much worse to Sheila, so much so that when she is upset, she doesn't go looking for her mother, but for "my father".

She is also kept off stage while Sheila confronts Gerald with having an affair with Eva as Daisy Renton. Although there are good dramatic reasons for removing all the other characters at this stage, so we can focus on Gerald and Sheila's relationship, Priestley also uses the absence symbolically. It symbolises her blindness once again – she misses everything that the family has done wrong because, metaphorically, she will always pretend it didn't happen anyway.

You should remember the irony of this blindness from the earlier section on names.

<u>Mrs Birling in Act 2</u>

When she re-enters, she again wishes to present a false front, *"Now Mrs Birling. Enters, briskly and self-confidently, quite out of key"* with the confessions we have just had.

Priestley wants us to know this is simply pretence when she responds to Sheila's alarm with a show, a pretence, *"affecting great surprise"*.

He immediately links this to her role as mother. We realise quite how distant she is when she refers to Sheila as "this child" instead of 'my child' or better still, 'my daughter'. Next, she attempts to dismiss Sheila as she would a "child", "I think you ought to go to bed".

Her Obsession with Social Status Makes her a Terrible Mother

In the conversation that follows Priestley reveals her obsession with social status. This is so paralysing that it even stops her having a relationship with her daughter, "don't contradict me like that", "what? Really, Sheila!"

He juxtaposes this with her snobbery towards Eva, "Girls of that class". He suggests that the urge to see the working class as less than human extends to placing everyone on a hierarchy, so that even members of her own family are less important and subservient to her. Perhaps Priestley uses this to illustrate to the ruling classes that their own snobbery damages their own lives, and their families' lives.

Again she attempts to maintain the pretence that Eric is not an alcoholic. Once Sheila has confirmed Eric is, she turns to Gerald, not to get at the truth, but to get a public denial. For her, the appropriate action is always to deny the truth if it is incriminating. However, Gerald doesn't side with her, and she retorts, "(*bitterly*) And this is the time you choose to tell me," meaning that he has allowed the truth to be exposed in public, rather than lie.

Priestley Makes her Seem Ridiculous

At this stage in the play Priestley begins to ridicule her, because her words become so inappropriate. For example, as Gerald begins to confess his affair with Daisy, rather than attack him for his betrayal of Sheila, her only daughter, she attacks his description of Alderman Meggarty's fat body as a "carcass", "there's no need to be disgusting". This is bitterly ironic, as betraying Sheila should be what she labels "disgusting".

Then she becomes disgusted at the Alderman's womanising, "*staggered*) well, really! Alderman Meggarty!" completely ignoring that her future son in law has done much worse. When he finally confesses, she can't even muster a proper protest, only offering a single word, "What?"

Eventually, when Gerald has finished his confession, she objects, "it's disgusting to me". Priestley gives us the impression that she is more upset about it becoming public knowledge than about the effect on her daughter. This is why he makes her emphasise the word "me", not caring how Sheila feels.

He Makes the Inspector Expose her Personality Before her Mistreatment of Eva
Birling and Gerald both tried to lie to The Inspector, but Mrs Birling takes this a step further by pretending not to recognise Eva from the photograph. Priestley makes The Inspector confront her with her lying, "you're not telling me the truth."

Her attempts to deny the facts are presented as childish, until The Inspector forces her to admit her influence denied Eva the charitable help she needed: "was it or was it not your influence?"

Priestley wants us to dislike her most as a character. Perhaps this is because she symbolises why the country needs a system of welfare. When the poor depend on charity for financial help, rather than government, the class system simply exploits them. The rich in Britain have a history of making a distinction between the deserving poor, and the undeserving poor. Priestley uses his unpleasant portrayal of Mrs Birling to attack the upper-class view that the poor might not deserve help: "she seemed to me not a good case."

Mrs Birling's Sin is Pride, Illustrated Through Social Snobbery
He attacks it further by getting Mrs Birling to explain why she did not think Eva had a good case. First, it is her snobbery: "it was simply a piece of gross impertinence – quite deliberate – and naturally that was one of the things that prejudiced me against her case."

Priestley gives her the word "prejudiced" to condemn her attitude in her own words. And he has already had Sheila ridicule the word "impertinence" in order to further make the audience dislike her.

Eva's final offence, in Sybil's eyes, is not that she was lying about being married, or called "Mrs Birling", but that she was behaving in a way that Mrs Birling would only accept of an upper-class woman, "She was claiming elaborate fine feelings and scruples that were simply absurd in a girl in her position." She simply can't believe that Eva, as someone who is working class, and therefore not "fine" would turn down money because it was stolen. Eva's greatest crime is therefore considering herself equal to the upper classes as a human being. This is the real reason Mrs Birling is so offended at Eva's choice of name, because it illustrates exactly that they are equal – they have the same name.

Priestley does this to symbolise his message, that we are all equal, all "of one body".

Because Mrs Birling is the only character to disagree with this belief, we can infer that Priestley wants us to be most angry at her. Many readers also see her as intended to be the most dislikeable character, and therefore the guiltiest, because she was Eva's last hope and still feels no guilt, "But I accept no blame for it at all."

But What if Mrs Birling is Right?
However, a counter argument to that is how Priestley reveals Eric's exploitation of Eva last, as though to emphasise that his actions were worse. There is also a further counter

argument. Eva could actually have accepted the stolen money. She could actually have accepted Eric's offer of marriage. And she certainly did tell the charity and Mrs Birling a number of lies:

- That she was called Mrs Birling.
- That she was married.
- That her husband had "deserted her".

So, in terms of the facts, Mrs Birling is quite right to say, "The girl had begun by telling us a pack of lies."

When Eva tells her that she wouldn't take stolen money, Sybil's reaction "all a lot of nonsense – I didn't believe a word of it" is not just snobbery. It is also a logical doubt to have given the lies which preceded it.

Another psychological problem for Mrs Birling to accept is that Eva would rather commit suicide than take the stolen money, or marry Eric, even though she describes him as "he didn't belong to her class, and was some drunken young idler".

When we begin to look at Eva's tragedy through this lens, Priestley appears to be suggesting that Eric has had a far greater effect on her committing suicide. It is not so much that Mrs Birling and her charity denied Eva help, as that they forced her to return to Eric.

Some readers think that Priestley makes The Inspector manipulate Mrs Birling into condemning her own son as an extra punishment for her sin of pride. The Inspector uses her own words about the "idle", "drunken" father to condemn Eric: "If the girl's death is due to anybody, then it's due to him."

But an alternative reading can argue that Mrs Birling's judgement here is in fact correct. The detail that Eva would rather commit suicide than return to Eric also suggests that Priestley thinks Eric's treatment of Eva is even worse than his mother's.

He still ends the act by ridiculing her deliberate blindness and unwillingness to face the truth. When Mrs Birling finally realise the irresponsible father is Eric, she exclaims, "I don't believe it. I won't believe it . . ." The emphasis on "won't" illustrates again her wilful blindness and self-deception. Through this Priestley is suggesting that the upper classes can only vote against socialism through deliberately not facing the facts, refusing to see the social injustice that he hopes the play will make visible to everyone.

Mrs Birling in Act Three

Priestley ridicules her self-deceit again, when she tries to deny it can be Eric who fathered Eva's child, but rehearsing an old lie she has already seen is a lie in Act 2, "Besides, you're not the type – you don't get drunk".

He then makes her leave the stage. This again symbolises her wilful blindness. She does not insist on staying to hear the details of the possible rape Eric commits against Eva. When she comes back on stage she is much more shocked at Eric for stealing money than forcing himself on Eva for sex, "(*Shocked*) Eric! You stole money?"

Because she represents the upper classes, Priestley uses this to symbolise how capitalism has corrupted their moral values. It is more shocking to steal money from a business than it is for her son to drunkenly force himself onto a working-class woman for sex.

At this point, Priestley removes The Inspector from the stage, as though this is a social experiment to see who will carry on learning once the teacher has left the room. We can see that The Inspector is most worried about Mrs Birling, which is why he delivers his parting message to her first, "Remember what you did, Mrs Birling." Perhaps as a sign that he fears she won't take responsibility for what she did, he repeats it, "Remember what you did."

Birling, Eric and Sheila all reply to The Inspector, and even Birling says he would "give thousands" to put right his mistake. Mrs Birling, however, says nothing. Priestley conveys here that she is the least likely to learn the lesson. Perhaps he also has in mind the women in his audience (given that the war was still being fought, they were likely to far outnumber the men in the audience). He wants to dramatise to his female audience how un-motherly, and unjust it would be to think like Mrs Birling. He needs her to be so objectionable so that Sheila can exist in counterpoint to her.

This counterpoint, or juxtaposition, tells his female audience that they would be much better and more likeable human beings if they followed Sheila's opinions, rather than Sybil's.

Arthur Birling

Birling in Act One
Priestley gives Birling the first words of the play, to establish him as patronising and condescending towards the working classes, "Giving us the port, Edna? That's right." Instead of asking for port, his question implies that Edna is too stupid to have noticed he wants it. His patronising "That's right" reminds us of a condescending teacher, anxious to prove they are superior to their pupil.

Birling Represents the Corruption of the Ruling Classes
This also symbolises how the upper classes view the working classes, literally as servants, to anticipate and meet their needs. To emphasise the corruption of the upper classes, Priestley begins with this ritual of drink – "port", which has twice the alcohol content of wine. Priestley is suggesting that the upper classes world view is distorted, literally impaired as brain function is impaired through drinking too much.

We have already seen how he is in a power struggle with his wife, and how he is excited at the business opportunity of marrying Sheila to Gerald Croft.

Priestley also represents him immediately as a corrupt capitalist, "when Crofts and Birlings are no longer competing but are working together – for lower costs and higher prices." Not only does he see his own daughter's marriage in terms of business, but he wants the two main businesses in Brumley to stop "competing". Remember, capitalism can only be fair when businesses compete – it makes them more efficient. The better workers produce more, so the business pays the best workers more, and everyone gets richer. However, Priestley makes Birling suggest that the businessmen need to get together to pay workers less, exploiting them and rigging the system.

Birling Discredits Capitalism
He uses Birling to discredit the capitalists, by linking their stupidity to the cause of The Depression in the 1930s, and to the two world wars of 1914 – 1918, and 1939 – 1945. Consequently, he speaks "as a hard-headed business man" to portray the selfishness of businessmen, but also to echo their greed in profiting from the war. Priestley gives him these words as they echo a famous accusation of profiteering made by Sir Stanley Baldwin, Prime Minister three times between the two world wars: *"hard-faced men who had done well out of the war"*. This is important to Priestley's audience, as Baldwin came from the same class as Gerald, being part of the nobility, an Earl. Priestley uses this allusion to show his audience that socialism is a kinder form of capitalism. He is not asking voters to revolt against capitalism, he is asking them to make capitalism fairer.

He discredits Birling, and therefore the ruling class, through Birling's confidence that certain events won't happen. He employs dramatic irony, because the 1945 audience would know each event did happen in history, between 1912 when the play was set and 1945 when it was performed.

He proclaims, "there's a lot of wild talk about possible labour trouble in the near future." The audience know of the general strike of 1926, and strikes which continued into the

1930s. But Priestley is also implying that going to war in 1914 was a capitalist tactic to stop strikes. War made everyone pull together for the war effort, and also killed off many of the strikers. A Marxist view would argue that war was therefore a practical, capitalist solution to rising costs and lower profits.

Many readers forget this. When they read "And we're in for a time of steadily increasing prosperity" they assume that this is also dramatic irony, as mass poverty in the 1930s demonstrated. However, Birling is referring to "We employers", the same business men who did very well out of the depression. Here, Birling is actually right.

War is Profitable to Capitalism
The irony is that Birling does not know he is right. He thinks that war is an enemy of capitalism, so he talks about there being no profit in war, "Everything to lose and nothing to gain by war." Using the language of profit and loss, however, shows that he doesn't fully understand capitalism. There was a huge profit in war, as the allusion to Stanley Baldwin made clear.

Priestley also uses this to illustrate another political point. It is fashionable for the rich to see themselves as deserving to be rich. They tell themselves their wealth is the result of talent or effort. They then tell themselves the poor deserve to be poor, because they have less talent and are less hard working. In these quotations, however, Priestley is suggesting the opposite. The rich stay rich not because of talent, but because they begin rich. Money is attracted to money. This is what "the interests of capital – are properly protected." Once you have "capital", you are "protected" against whatever is going on in the rest of society.

Next, he makes Birling dismiss war, "And I say there isn't a chance of war. The world's developing so fast that it'll make war impossible." Notice how he starts so many sentences with "And". This portrays him as childlike, and not having constructed his argument properly. Priestley builds on this by making him list all the reasons the world is "developing so fast":

> "aeroplanes that will be able to go anywhere. And look at the way the auto-mobile's making headway – bigger and faster all the time. And then ships."

However, to the audience in 1945, these very advances in the plane, engine speed of vehicles and size of ships are exactly what made possible the exportation of war to the 'world' in two world wars. Priestley does this to suggest that this capitalist development of technology is what made the exportation of war to world war possible.

Priestley Hates War More Than He Hates Capitalism
It is important to remember this. Most readers simply assume Priestley is protesting about the inequalities in society caused by capitalism. But that would be to forget The Inspector's final words, about a lesson taught in "fire and blood and anguish". Priestley wants to show how this brand of capitalism inevitably leads to war. That is his real beef with capitalism!

The other form of dramatic irony points to Birling's hubris (excessive pride or self-confidence) so the Titanic is "unsinkable, absolutely unsinkable. That's what you've got to keep your eye on, facts like that, progress like that". But, the Titanic is itself a metaphor for the ruling classes who, like the ship, have "every luxury". Although it seems that the ruling classes will once more triumph in the general election, with an overwhelming vote for the Conservative party, Priestley is asking his audience to see this as overconfidence. To add to that, we might imagine the iceberg that sinks it as the working classes, "millions of Eva Smiths and John Smiths" who now have a voice and, more crucially, suffrage, a vote. He makes the point even more sarcastically by making Birling assert that 1940 will be a time of peace, "a world that'll have forgotten all these capital versus labour agitations and all these silly little war scares".

Birling Represents the Patriarchy

Next Priestley wants to portray him as part of the patriarchy, in order to discredit the gender roles of Edwardian society. He tells Gerald "Lady Croft – while she doesn't object to my girl – feels you might have done better for yourself socially." He doesn't name Sheila, but refers to her more as a possession, "my girl". A further effect of women having so little power is that they fight to acquire it through marriage and class. This is why Priestley decides it isn't Sir Croft who will object to the marriage, but Lady Croft, to point out how women are so damaged they end up supporting the patriarchal society which has denied them equality in the first place.

Birling is Obsessed with Social Status

Priestley presents Birling as a symbol of the patriarchal society. It begins with his smoking a "cigar", which doesn't serve the plot, but points to his status as head of the family, and in Priestley's day would be a phallic representation of masculinity. He immediately matches this with an objectification of Sheila. He comments on Gerald's mother's view of Sheila, "while she doesn't object to my girl – feels you might have done better for yourself socially." The possessive "my girl" instead of 'Sheila' portrays her as a pawn Birling is using to do better for himself "socially", as well as through a business alliance.

Birling is of course socially obsessed, even buying the same "port" as "Sir Croft", and confides in Gerald that he is probably going to receive a "knighthood", so Priestley can highlight his desperation to climb the social hierarchy. So ambitious is he that he calls it "just a knighthood", so we imagine he longs for greater honours.

Priestley emphasises this by having Birling explain the significance of clothing to women, "not only something to make 'em look prettier – but – well, a sort of sign or token of their self-respect". This ought to be ridiculous, given all the other discredited "facts" he tells us. But, in a bitter irony, he is describing a social truth of 1912, and perhaps 1945. Society really does judge women by their appearance, and their status by the brands they wear. (Next time you are attracted to a particular brand, ask if you too are being exploited by the patriarchy!)

Birling is desperate to climb the social hierarchy. He references how he was "Lord Mayor" and that he is in line for honours, "Just a knighthood, of course". The use of "Just" reveals how ambitious he truly is.

Birling's Capitalism Summons the Inspector

Having established that Birling represents all capitalists and, symbolically, that all capitalists are sexist, hubristic (over confident, remember) and perhaps stupid, Priestley now makes him utter the words which summon The Inspector:

> "you'd think everybody has to look after everybody else ... community and all that nonsense. But ... that a man has to mind his own business and look after himself and his own"

Giving Birling these opinions, attacking socialism, is an ironic device. Because we reject Birling's earlier views, we now reject his attack on socialism, and instead begin to question capitalism.

In terms of the drama, Priestley will later point out the significance of these words in summoning The Inspector, as we have already seen, and The Inspector therefore arrives to convert us to socialism.

Birling is the first character to be confronted by The Inspector. Some might argue that he is therefore most responsible for Eva's tragedy, as he began it. He had her sacked when, in his own words, she was due a promotion, "A good worker too...the foreman...was ready to promote her".

Social Class is More Damaging to Society Than Capitalism

However, as we have seen, this sacking actually led to a better job at Milwards. In this way, capitalism is not the direct cause of her tragedy. Social class, and the immorality of the upper classes, however, is responsible.

Birling feels able to justify this cruelty by referring to how much paying his employees would cost the business, "Well it's my duty to keep labour costs down" rather than increase them by "twelve percent". Of course, while this seems cruel, it is also true. By 1945, as you will see later in the guide, Britain had lost its monopoly on the cotton trade, precisely because foreign competitors could pay their workers much less. Priestley understands Birling's view on wages, and knows many in his audience will share it, which is why he has worked so hard to discredit everything else about him. He hopes this will make the audience more likely to question their own belief about fair wages.

Priestley also uses Birling quite subtly to criticise the upper classes. Birling has become successful through business, he wasn't born into privilege. This is the opposite of his son, Eric, who he now criticises, "That's something this public-school-and-varsity life you've had doesn't seem to teach you." Even Birling is critical of the effect of being brought up as part of the ruling classes. This symbolises his message to his wealthy audience, a warning to stop trying to climb the social hierarchy, and instead make society fairer. Why pursue higher social status when it will only damage your character?

We see that most when we find out how Gerald and Eric are most responsible for Eva's tragedy.

Birling is the Enemy of Socialism

Once the Inspector has entered, Birling is polite, even if a little "impatient". Priestley highlights how Birling personifies the enemy of socialism, "If we were all responsible for everything that happened to everybody we'd had anything to do with, it would be very awkward, wouldn't it?" Priestley uses irony to make Birling condemn himself with his own words.

Despite the apparent socialist view expressed by The Inspector, Birling expects him to agree that they should only pay workers "neither more nor less" than is paid at other companies, so he explains that he refused the strikers' wage demands, "I refused, of course." He is visibly "surprised" when The Inspector asks "why?"

Up to this point he describes his female workers as "girls" rather than women. When he discusses not giving them a wage rise, he now refers to them in the abstract, as "labour", in language which refuses to treat them as human, "it's my duty to keep labour costs down." Priestley shows through this use of "duty" that capitalism is like a religion to Birling, demanding his loyalty. Priestley probably does this because he knows many in his audience will share Birling's viewpoint.

This is why he portrays Birling as arrogant here. He decides to sack the "ringleaders" himself, so we can see an element of enjoyment in his actions. Then his description of the strike is sneering and superior, as a "Pitiful affair". Again, Priestley uses irony to expose him, because pity is exactly what Birling was missing in his sacking of the strike leaders.

Birling is a Ruthless Parent

Priestley also ensures that his parenting style is just as ruthless. We have already seen that his main interest in Sheila is the business and social alliance she will provide with her marriage to Gerald. When she now enters, to find out about Eva, Birling tells her patronisingly to "run along". Eric's drinking is probably caused by returning home from university, where his father has refused to give him any "responsibility", and he embarrasses Eric about this in front of The Inspector. Priestley contrasts this with Gerald's father, "Sir George", who has happily gone "abroad", probably leaving Gerald in charge of the business.

Perhaps Priestley also shows how little interest he has in his children when he leaves them alone with The Inspector when he knows that Sheila is next to be questioned. Instead he insists on having a conversation off stage with "my wife", who is clearly more important to him.

Birling in Act Two

Birling remains off stage for a long time in Act Two, instead sending his wife on stage to deal with The Inspector. Partly Priestley must do this to allow The Inspector to focus on characters who have not been exposed yet. However, he reveals Birling's patronising and domineering manner. Not only has he dismissed Sheila, while off stage he has been telling Eric, a grown man, "to go to bed".

Birling Exploits Sheila for Social and Financial Profit

Birling continues to patronise Sheila and reveals the cruelty of this patriarchal society. He expects Sheila to accept Gerald's affair with Daisy Renton, and only tries to get Sheila to leave when Gerald mentions "women of the town." He simply expects that, because Gerald is an upper-class man, he will be paying for sex with these prostitutes. Yet, far from being critical of this, he still expects Sheila to marry Gerald. Removing her from this confession will simply make it psychologically easier for her to ignore, pretending that her future husband is loyal to her.

We see how cynical Birling is when Sheila mentions Alderman Meggarty sexually assaulted a girl she knows, who "only escaped with a torn blouse". Birling exclaims "Sheila!" to tell her off for mentioning it, as he expects her to be more loyal to influential men of her class, and simply put up with their predatory behaviour.

When he hears about Gerald's own sexual infidelity to Sheila, he corruptly tries to make her accept the status quo, that infidelity is exactly what she should expect from her fiancé, "Now, Sheila, I'm not defending him. But you must understand that a lot of young men…"

Because he is so obsessed with his status in the patriarchy, he demands that The Inspector stop being "offensive" and remember he is a "public man". His language emphasises his male power. Even when he talks about Eric, who he discovers at the end of the act is the father of Eva's baby, he highlights his own status at the expense of his son's: "you're not trying to tell us that – that my boy – is mixed up in this?" Although this sounds paternal, it is also patronising to call Eric a mere "boy". Priestley does this to show how damaging this patriarchal society is. In fact, we can infer that this oppression by his father, refusing to give him the responsibilities of adulthood, has led to Eric's erratic behaviour and drinking.

Birling in Act Three

A Patriarchal Society Needs Women to be Kept in Ignorance
Priestley begins act three keen to show us that Birling and his wife are united against their children. Birling consequently begins by admonishing Sheila, with "that's enough" and criticising her lack of "loyalty". Similarly, he yells "explosively" at Eric when refusing his request for a drink.

Priestley also uses Birling to emphasise the inequality of the patriarchal social rules which he enforces. Consequently, he demands that Sheila take her mother out, so that neither woman has to hear how Eric has impregnated Eva. Although this might be seen as an attempt to protect the women in his family, this isn't merely patronising. If they don't hear the full details, there will be some aspects of Eric's behaviour that Birling hopes to be able to keep secret from them.

Priestley is careful to have the women off stage when Eric reveals his probable rape of Eva. This will prove vitally important with the second death at the end of the act. If Eric and Sheila have learned the lesson, then it may be that the future will change. However, history tells Priestley's audience that it doesn't change, the lessons aren't learned and the mistakes of The First World War are repeated in The Second World War. Priestley makes it easier for Eric not to learn this lesson by making sure that no one else knows about the worst of his crimes, so that in future he will be able to forget his predatory behaviour. If others don't know about it, they can't mention it to him.

Priestley also hints that Eric will not be able to resist his father's overbearing control, when Eric tells Birling why he stole rather than come to his father for help, "you're not the kind of father a chap could go to when he's in trouble".

Violence Toward Women is Inevitable in a Patriarchy
When Eric turns on Sybil for her refusal to help Eva, Birling appears to be about to strike Eric, "Why, you hysterical young fool – get back – or I'll-" We might also infer that Eric has learned this level of violence from his father, rather than just because he is drunk. Either way, Priestley is highlighting the physical violence inherent in male behaviour, and linking it to the need for men to assert their status in the hierarchy. He deliberately contrasts this with The Inspector's behaviour, which is authoritative without violence, "(taking charge, masterfully) Stop!"

At this stage, Birling also feels he has learned The Inspector's lesson, and claims he would "give thousands" to bring Eva back.

Birling Blames Anyone But Himself
However, we can see this is insincere, as his immediate reaction when The Inspector leaves is to blame Eric, "you're the one I blame". His next thought is again to worry about his status, "I was almost certain of a knighthood". Priestley uses this to symbolise how the class system devalues human life, as Birling forgets about Eva's death, and completely denies responsibility, "There's every excuse for what both your mother and I did".

Discovering Goole is not a real inspector simply strengthens this view, and "makes all the difference" to Birling. The difference has nothing to do with his guilt, but his relief that there will be no "inquest" and no "scandal".

Priestley ensures we dislike him here by making him claim that he would normally have "seen through" the "hoax" from the start. This is intended to remind us that Birling's world view is built on self-deception, the capitalist self-deception that one's "duty" is not "everybody" but just to "oneself".

Birling Loves Wealth and Status More Than He Loves his Children

He also makes Birling turn on Eric, who has lost a lover, but also an unborn child. Birling is so unsympathetic that he does not even mention this. He simply wants revenge on the imposter, The Inspector, exclaiming, "Now it's our turn", so that his son's feelings count for nothing. His only concern about Eric is that he pay him back "that money you stole". Here we can see that the desire for revenge extends to his own son: after all, £50 is a tiny sum to Birling.

This fixation on money is also another way to remind us that Birling still represents the businessmen and capitalism. Now, even his language choices to describe the "hoax" borrow from a capitalist register, when he claims it was "Nothing but an elaborate sell!" Priestley also uses heavy irony here, when Birling claims "Nobody likes to be sold as badly as that". For him, this is just a metaphor: as we have seen for Eva, and Daisy Renton, it is much more literal, as she has literally been "sold" to or rented by Gerald, then Eric.

Priestley reminds us that Birling's cruelty as a capitalist also makes him cruel to his own family. Consequently, just as he dismisses Eric's emotions and focuses on money, now he dismisses Sheila's feelings and focuses on wealth, "Look, you'd better ask Gerald for that ring you gave back to him, hadn't you?" We understand from this that Birling's love of his family is far weaker than his love of wealth and status.

Birling's last words of the play directed at his children are simply intended to mock and humiliate them as "the famous younger generation" who "can't take a joke". These of course are campaigning words from Priestley. He wants the younger generation to reject their parents' view, and vote for a "socialist" society. Another way this achieves that aim is that he encourages them to look at their own parents, who are the same generation as Eric and Sheila, and realise that they too had their chance to learn the lesson of World War One. It points to the real tragedy of the play, that Eric and Sheila did not act on that lesson, and history repeated itself, just as it does with the phone call at the final curtain: "a police inspector is on his way here…"

Are you ready for more?

Context and Assessment Objective 3

The Labour Party Manifesto Context

Priestley stood as an independent MP in 1945. We can see that he was passionate about politics because he believed in making a difference to working people, and because he wanted to change the way people thought about each other, and about the future.

The obsession with time which we see in An Inspector Calls is also an obsession with the future. This is shared by the whole country.

The Labour Party Manifesto, as we would call it now, was called:

> **"Let Us Face the Future:**
> **A Declaration of Labour Policy for the Consideration of the Nation"**

We could probably argue that "Let us Face the Future" would work perfectly as an alternative title for this play. We could definitely argue that the moral lesson Priestley wants to teach is about the ruling classes facing up to their actions in order to build a better future for "us", for everyone, not just themselves.

The following are all quotations from the Labour Party manifesto which are directly relevant to An Inspector Calls and Priestley's socialism. This is helpful for us in two ways.

Firstly, it shows us how in tune this play, and Priestley's views were with people at the time.

Secondly, it shows how voters did not know this. Most people were expecting another Conservative victory. Who would bet against Churchill, who many saw as the saviour of the country during the war? Most socialists were convinced Churchill would still be the people's choice to lead them in the peace, just after the war. Priestley felt there was still a lot of persuading to do.

In fact there wasn't.

The 1945 Election Result

With 48 per cent of the vote, Labour gained a Parliamentary majority of 146 seats, the largest in post-war British history.

The swing to Labour of 12 points is the highest there has been in any election since the war, in the biggest landslide victory.

Conservative numbers in the House of Commons nearly halved, dropping from 387 to 197. The Liberal Party was reduced to only 12 seats.

What Does the Play Have in Common With <u>Let Us Face the Future</u>?

Accompanying each quotation is an explanation of how it is relevant to our study of the play.

1. 'The gallant men and women in the Fighting Services, in the Merchant Navy, Home Guard and Civil Defence, in the factories and in the bombed areas - they deserve and must be assured a happier future than faced so many of them after the last war. Labour regards their welfare as a sacred trust.'

Here we can see Priestley's concerns with welfare for all, particularly in his depiction of how Mrs Birling's charity refuses to do a proper job. We can also see how important the future is in the language and thoughts of the time. Just as in the play, the manifesto uses deliberately Christian imagery, such as "sacred trust" and links this to socialism, seeing "welfare as a sacred trust".

The rhythm of the sentences is also much like The Inspector's in his final message:

"One Eva Smith has gone – but there are millions and millions and millions of Eva Smiths and John Smiths still left with us, with their lives, their hopes and fears, their suffering and chance of happiness, all intertwined with our lives, and what we think and say and do. We don't live alone. We are members of one body. We are responsible for each other."

The rhythm is created by repetition in both cases, and in both cases it drives the political message home.

2. 'So the "hard-faced men who had done well out of the war" were able to get the kind of peace that suited themselves. The people lost that peace. And when we say "peace" we mean not only the Treaty, but the social and economic policy which followed the fighting.'

The enemy therefore are the rich business owners who made money from The First World War. The description of these as 'hard men' is deliberately echoed in Birling's words, "I'm taking as a hard headed, practical man of business". Priestley is deliberately using the language of the Labour Party manifesto, to turn it into a drama his audience can relate to.

3. 'Great economic blizzards swept the world in those years. The great inter-war slumps were not acts of God or of blind forces. They were the sure and certain result of the concentration of too much economic power in the hands of too few men. These... had and... felt no responsibility to the nation.'

This need to be 'responsible' is at the heart of The Inspector's teaching. It also sets out a clear warning, just as The Inspector does. Here the warning instead of The Inspector's "fire and blood and anguish", is 'blizzards' or economic hardship.

This is presented as being entirely because of the ruling classes acting 'in the interest of their own', which is of course what Gerald, the Crofts and the Birlings represent. Again, this is echoed in Birling's words, a "man has to look after himself".

It is also significant that the Labour Party is clearly attacking men, not women. It is "men" who have "too much economic power". This is a theme which Priestley picks up. It is why Eva, the victim, is female, and it is also why Gerald and Eric are her worst abusers.

WHAT THE ELECTION WILL BE ABOUT

4. *'We must prevent another war, and that means we must have such an international organisation as will give all nations real security against future aggression.'*

But, it is not just the economic argument of a 'fair share' for all that the Labour Party are after. Just as in the play, a main concern is the prevention of future war. **It is very easy to forget that this is a main focus of the play.**

5. *'But there are certain so-called freedoms that Labour will not tolerate: freedom to exploit other people; freedom to pay poor wages and to push up prices for selfish profit; freedom to deprive the people of the means of living full, happy, healthy lives.'*

Priestley dramatises this directly in the conversation Eric has with his father about his sacking of Eva after the strike. 'I think it's a shame. We try for the highest profits, why shouldn't they try for the highest wages.' And as Sheila says, 'they're people'.

6. These words could have been spoken directly by The Inspector:

'the Labour Party will put the community first and the sectional interests of private business after.'

This is why Priestley gives Birling the line dismissing 'community and all that nonsense.'

INDUSTRY IN THE SERVICE OF THE NATION

7. *'Millions of working and middle class people went through the horrors of unemployment and insecurity. It is not enough to sympathise with these victims: we must develop an acute feeling of national shame - and act.'*

These again could be The Inspector's words. They perfectly sum up Priestley's purpose in writing the play, calling people to action, asking the ruling classes to feel 'shame'. Priestley deliberately uses the same language when Eric tells his parents:

"Well, I don't blame you. But don't forget I'm ashamed of you as well – yes both of you."

EDUCATION AND RECREATION

8. *"And, above all, let us remember that the great purpose of education is to give us individual citizens capable of thinking for themselves."*

Priestley's desire as a teacher can be reflected here. The Inspector asks Eric and Sheila to think for themselves, and at the end of the play it appears that they have. This is another reason that Priestley leaves his audience with so many questions. The audience have to think for themselves to answer the questions that the ending poses. Who has died? Are they all responsible? Who is the new inspector?

How Should You Use These Ideas?

1. They will help you argue that it is a deeply political play, with a strong socialist message.
2. That it is a play clearly of its time, tapping into the ideas of the time, as well as helping to shape them.
3. That it is so much of its time that Priestley deliberately uses some of the same language as the manifesto, as though he has internalised or remembered parts of it.
4. That Priestley's life and his play were not separate. He wrote it as a campaigning play, at the same time as he decided to campaign directly in politics, standing as an MP.
5. That the language choices and rhythms of the manifesto are very similar to longer speeches of The Inspector.

The Great Unrest: Strikes Between 1910 and 1912

National strikes live a long time in the national memory. Ask your parents and grandparents about the miners strikes in the 1980s, or the miners strikes of the 1970s which led to massive power cuts and 'the three-day week' to see what I mean.

These were nothing compared to the strikes at the time of <u>An Inspector Calls</u>.

The Great Unrest

- From 1910, worker unrest began to grow in number and size.
- In 1911-12, as many as 41 million days were lost to strikes.
- In 1911, a walk out by porters with the Cheshire and Lancashire railway company led to the first ever national strike. This led to the foundation of the National Union of Railwayman.

This was a threatening development for business men like Birling – if the mill workers developed a national union, he and other owners would not be able to run a cartel, offering deliberately lower wages.

As Birling points out, "We were paying the usual rates and if they didn't like those rates, they could go and work somewhere else". This means all the factory owners are paying Eva and the thousands of other women who work in their factories a wage that is only just enough to get by, with barely any savings.

Eric retorts with, "It isn't if you can't go and work somewhere else" because if workers can move jobs for higher wages, they will.

In a fair capitalist system, this should not happen. The Birlings and Crofts and other factory owners would compete for workers, and therefore wages would be higher as they compete to attract better staff. But, if the owners get together and *all* agree to set lower wages, better staff have nowhere to go, and wages stay low. This is called a cartel and is in most instances illegal.

- Often these strikes became violent, with widespread vandalism of tracks and stations.

- During a city-wide general strike in Liverpool, the government was so concerned about violence that they sent a warship to the Mersey. Troops also shot two strikers when they broke up a crowd of 80,000.

- In Llanelli, soldiers opened fire on a crowd, killing two workmen. Significantly, Winston Churchill was the Home Secretary at the time, and had ordered the sending of troops.

So, when The Inspector leaves with his warning that the Birlings must learn their lesson "And I tell you that the time will soon come when, if men will not learn that lesson, then they well be taught it in fire and blood and anguish" he does of course mean war. But, he also means industrial unrest which, as his audience knew, would certainly lead to workers being killed by their own soldiers.

- 1914 saw a national miners strike, with over 100,000 going on strike in Yorkshire alone.

- In London, coal deliveries stopped, and people ended up paying to transport coal for their fireplaces by taxi.

- Workers became more powerful so union membership rose from 2.5 million in 1910 to 4.1 million in 1914, 27% of all workers.

- The unions were patriotic. They agreed to call a halt to the strikes during the war, and of course hundreds of thousands of union members were killed in the battlefields.

Many in Priestley's audience in 1945 wouldn't just remember the strikes. They would remember how The First World War stopped them winning significant rights for workers. And of course, in 1945, it had all happened again. Like the voters, Priestley did not want the ruling classes to simply carry on as they had before, making larger profits while their workers existed on low wages.

What Caused The Great Unrest?
Britain faced new challenges from abroad. In 1873 Britain was the largest economic power in the world, having an astonishing 31.8% of the world's total manufacturing business. By 1913 Britain had been overtaken by the USA and Germany, and now produced only 14% of world manufacturing.

In 1860, Britain produced 60% of the world's total coal. In 1912, that figure had dropped to only 24%. In 1870 Britain produced 49% of the world's iron, but in 1912 it had dropped to only 12%. (source https://www.marxist.com/1912-the-great-unrest.htm)

One effect of this competition from abroad was to reduce prices that business could charge. They therefore wanted to pay workers as little as possible.

This was also a time when the rich got richer. Britain developed banking and finance during this time, bringing back huge amounts of money from the British Empire. For example, money coming in from India alone accounted for two fifths of the balance of trade deficit.

British investment abroad in 1913 accounted for £4 billion. The USA, Germany, France, Belgium and Holland combined had only £5.5 billion invested abroad. This meant that British investors made more money by investing abroad rather than in Britain, and so

Britain's own manufacturing and industry declined, with owners like the Birlings less inclined to improve equipment and factories.

The 1911 Census shows that the richest 1% of the population controlled 70% of the nation's wealth. In 1914, 4% of the population owned 90% of the nation's wealth. Between 1900 and 1910 food prices increased faster than wages, so real earnings, the amount your wages were worth, dropped by 10%.

Many historians argue that the country would have seen very violent civil unrest if the war had not interrupted the mood of national protest in 1914.

Why is this important to your understanding of the play?
Let's look again at The Inspector's warning:

> "We don't live alone. We are members of one body. We are responsible for each other. And I tell you that the time will soon come when, if men will not learn that lesson, then they well be taught it in fire and blood and anguish."

This is actually very odd. How can The First World War be caused by the rich not being "responsible for each other", but instead trying to make huge profits while keeping wages as low as possible? How does that make sense – there's no connection between that and war, is there?

Well, here's the connection. How did the government stop all the unrest, the strikes, the threat to business? They went to war. They began with volunteers enlisting, but then conscripted. This meant every male had to go to war once they were 18. And of course the businessmen, and the rich running the country didn't go to war. They were too old to be conscripted. So, rich men profited from the deaths of 700,000 British soldiers.

It might feel a bit far-fetched to say that this was the only reason Britain went to war with Germany in 1914, but many historians see it as the main reason – it made economic sense. A Marxist interpretation would say that the rich ruling classes went to war to maintain their own profits. Yes, this resulted in many more of their own sons being killed (as they formed the officer class). But they saw it as a price worth paying. That's how brutal capitalism is.

In 1945, the Labour Party manifesto certainly saw The First World War as part of a wider business opportunity, 'So the "hard-faced men who had done well out of the war"'. The use of the quotation "hard-faced men" implies that they deliberately sacrificed men's lives in order to support the war.

It is also deliberately echoed by Priestley in Birling's words, as "a hard headed, practical man of business". Priestley wants his audience to make the connection. Priestley wasn't quoting the manifesto – both he and the manifesto were quoting a famous Prime Minister, Stanley Baldwin, who described many businessmen who had become MPs this way in 1918: **"A lot of hard-faced men who look as if they had done very well out of the war."**

Most of his audience would get this reference.

And, what would have happened to the textile factory owners like Birling and Crofts, and the steel producers, and the manufacturers of all kinds during the war? The demand for everything they made would have skyrocketed. How many uniforms do you have to make for an army of 6 million? How many bullets, guns, tanks, planes and ships did businessmen make money from?

All of them.

And the Labour Party manifesto also made clear that these same businessmen continued to make money after the war, they "were able to get the kind of peace that suited themselves. The people lost that peace. And when we say "peace" we mean not only the Treaty, but the social and economic policy which followed the fighting."

What Happens Between the Wars (1918-1939) and Why Does this Matter?

So, you are J B Priestley. You are going to stand as an MP, because you are desperate for a socialist government, one that looks after its people with a welfare state, a free national health service, support for the unemployed, a fair wage for workers, jobs for women, and an end to future world wars.

You want to write a play which explores your values, shows people what you believe in and is dramatic and memorable.

Why on earth would you set a play in 1912, instead of just before this war, 1939, or even during this war?

There are lots of possible reasons. Which ones best fit your reading of the play?
1. He wants to teach his audience about what he thinks are the root causes of both world wars: the selfishness and greed of its ruling classes. By drawing a parallel with The First World War he can make the case that a change of government is even more urgent – it should have happened in 1918, and didn't. Let's make sure it happens in 1945.

2. He wants to remind his audience of the incredible social change which happened between the wars – women getting the vote, the rise in trade unions, the General Strike of 1926, the Great Depression – as this will remind them of the conflict they should avoid by voting for what he sees as a fairer society.

3. 1912 has great personal significance for him – it is the year he was first published as a writer. In some ways, he is looking back over his own adult lifetime to try to understand what has happened in Britain since then.

4. By comparing his contemporary society of 1945 to the old Edwardian one of 1912, he can make the case that conservative politics, which he sees as looking after the rich and business owners, is out dated – it is time for society to move on and evolve.

5. Priestley fought in The First World War, and was one of over 5 million survivors who were culturally programmed not to talk about their wartime experience.

Why Didn't Writers Talk About World War One
Writers simply didn't write about The First World War. There are lots of theories as to why soldiers found it so hard to talk about. Don't forget that Priestley was a soldier for the whole of the war. Many more of his friends would have died than someone joining up half way through, so whatever affected most soldiers to prevent them talking about the war probably affected him far more.

This could be one reason why Priestley destroyed his book of poetry which he wrote during the war. Part of the reason could be that he no longer liked the poems. But far more likely is that they contained memories which he felt should not be spoken about or shared.

Here is a quotation from Julia Walker, writing for The British Library, in her 2014 Article: The Silence After the War

https://www.bl.uk/world-war-one/articles/the-silence-after-the-war

"Henri Barbusse's graphic account of trench life, Under Fire (1916), was widely read on both sides of the Front, with a 1917 reviewer in The Manchester Guardian noting that generally 'the "horrors of war" are taken for granted but ... mercifully concealed.'"

This indicates the culture of silence at the time – people at home wanted to be spared the graphic descriptions of war. This is one reason why Priestley only hints at it, but never describes it.

One of the earliest accounts of the war was by T. E. Lawrence: The Seven Pillars of Wisdom, published in 1922. Demand was so low that only 8 copies were printed then. Later it would become much more successful, and his wartime exploits were turned into a David Lean film, Lawrence of Arabia.

Most novels that dealt with the violence of the war were not published until ten years after it:
- Remarque's All Quiet On The Western Front (1929)
- Robert Graves' Goodbye To All That (1929)
- Charles Edmonds' A Subaltern's War (1929)
- Helen Z Smith's Not So Quiet (1930)
- Frederic Manning's Her Privates We (1930),
- Siegfried Sassoon's Memoirs of an Infantry Officer (1930)

"are a few of over 60 books on the war that were published in these two years."

This also suggests that the outpouring of writing worked as a kind of catharsis – writers wanted to get it out of their system, so that the memories could be forgotten. What the soldiers actually wanted was to get rid of the memories of war. This could be another reason why Priestley avoided writing about it.

Robert Graves commented about Goodbye to All That: 'once this has been settled in my mind and written down and published it need never be thought about again.' If he is typical, it adds weight to the theory that soldiers simply wanted to put the war behind them. This is why they are all published in a two year window.

We could argue that Priestley sees this as damaging. If it is part of the culture to forget the war, it is a small step to creating a culture which forgets about the causes of the war. The structure of the play, with the two deaths of Eva symbolising the two world wars, strongly suggests that Priestley needs his audience to think about these causes.

The problem is, if he writes directly about the war, his audience will metaphorically flinch and turn away, as it has become part of the culture to turn away from thinking about the war. His solution to that is merely to allude to it, and not mention it directly.

So, when Priestley makes The Inspector say:

"I tell you that the time will soon come when, if men will not learn that lesson, then they well be taught it in fire and blood and anguish"

he is acknowledging the British impulse not to talk directly about the war.

So his warning is subtle. He is willing to remove The Inspector after Act 2, so he doesn't have to spell out the atrocities of war which will lead to that "fire and blood and anguish". But, the message continues, that won't really help. If the ruling classes don't learn the lesson, they won't just have to talk about it, they'll have to live it. This is "the lesson".

Why Does Priestley Choose a Textile Factory for Eva to Work in, Rather than a Different Industry?

1. Priestley's first job was in the textile trade – he could simply be following the advice writers have always had – write about what you know.

2. He needed his victim to be female, because he wants to show how the British patriarchy damages women even more than men. Because textile factories employed so many women, it was a natural setting.

3. The textile industries most represented what he saw as wrong with capitalist society. In 1912, Britain owned most of the world's textile trade. But, perhaps uniquely, these massive businesses were controlled not by companies, but mainly by families. It allows Priestley to attack the Birlings as a family, but also makes it easier for his audience to see that they don't just symbolise the ruling classes – this one family is already a large percentage of the ruling class.

4. He needed an industry that had once been completely dominant and was now in complete decline. This helps his message, that the "hard headed, practical man of business" like Birling is actually destroying the economy of the country. Of all the manufacturing industries, textiles is the one where Britain had arguably experienced the biggest decline by 1945. It had arguably been Britain's most successful industry in 1912.

Some Astonishing Facts About Britain and its Industry

The quotations in this section come from World Textile Industry by John Singelton. "Three textile enterprises qualified for membership of the world's 98 largest industrial companies in 1912. Ranked by market capitalisation of equity, J and P Coats, the British sewing thread producer, valued at $300.8 million, was the third largest industrial firm in the world.

The other leading textile corporations, in 1912, were American Woolen (63rd, $39.6 million) and the Britain's Fine Cotton Spinners and Doublers Association (72nd, $34.4 million)... J and P Coats's position was all the more remarkable because the Coats family continued to play a significant part in its direction."

Knowing that these companies kept their family ownership and structures helps us see why Priestley has chosen them as his models for capitalism. These are companies which lived up exactly to Birling's viewpoint, a man looking "after himself" and "his family", at the expense of millions of workers.

The proposed merger between Birling's and Crofts is not just a theoretical one. In 1929, Lancashire firms merged to form the Lancashire Cotton Corporation, with 10 million spindles!

Of course, it is unlikely to be a coincidence that Crofts is such a similar sounding name to Coats, and many of his audience would make the connection.

A further reason to use the Birlings and the textile trade is what happened to it after 1920, along with much of British manufacturing which had led the world. Capitalism could quite clearly be shown to be failing, because of Britain's sharp decline in output.

Priestley doesn't bore us with figures like these. Instead he tries to show that capitalists are stupid. This is why he gives Birling the speech about the Titanic being "absolutely unsinkable". The Titanic therefore becomes a metaphor for British manufacturing industry, which had seemed unsinkable in 1870, still seemed impressive in 1913, and had been well and truly sunk by 1945.

In 1870 Britain had the largest economy in the world. Look what happened by 1913 (Source http://www.marxist.com/1912-the-great-unrest.htm)

Percentage Distribution of the World's Manufacturing Production 1870 and 1913

	(% of world total)	
	1870	1913
USA	23.3	35.8
Germany	13.2	15.7
U.K	31.8	14.0
France	10.3	6.4
Russia	3.7	5.5

So, the textile trade was probably Britain's most successful industry in 1912, at a time when other manufacturing was being overtaken by Germany and America.

These figures also add evidence to The First World War having an economic cause. Not only would it strengthen British manufacturing, it would also weaken its main European competitor, Germany.

How to Write an Exam Essay

This is a classic <u>An Inspector Calls</u> question:
How Does Priestley Show the Conflict Between the Younger and Older Generations?

I am going to show you two versions of a complete answer. The first is an excellent revision technique. Simply copy the examiner's indicative comment and frame your entire essay around that. Initially, this might take you longer than 45 minutes. But that doesn't matter. In this exercise, you are trying to learn what the examiner wants. This is important, as the examiner will want much of this indicative comment *whatever the question*.

Once you have tried this approach with a number of essay questions you will know the examiner's mind – you'll know what they are expecting in any question. So, although the essay is about the generations, it will also show you the key ideas to write about in an essay on all the characters.

Then I am going to show you how to take that 1000 word essay, and reduce it to under 700, but still gain a grade 9.

Enough chat. Let's make a start.

Typical Exam Board Indicative Content
The first thing you need to know is that any interpretation will be "valid" so long as it is supported with evidence.

These are the four things a 'personal' response will do:

1. <u>Begin with the author's purpose</u>
2. *Link the author's purpose to symbolism*
3. **Refer to the characters as a construct**
4. Propose an alternative interpretation

<u>AO1: The Ability to Quote and Explore Interpretations, Including Personal Response</u>

The indicative content might refer to Sheila, Eric and Gerald's reactions to The Inspector.

<u>If the Inspector's voice and views are a proxy for Priestley's socialist message, that "we are all one body" and "responsible for each other", then the younger generation are a proxy for his audience in 1945.</u>

Sheila is the most impressed by The Inspector, and he remarks that "we often do (make an impression) on the young ones". She observes that "he inspected us alright" and welcomes his teaching, that we must look after everyone, *all the "John Smiths and Eva Smiths", symbolising the working classes.*

Priestley creates these characters, not just because they are young, but also ***because they will have most power in this capitalist society***. Sheila and Eric will inherit the Birlings' wealth and status, and Gerald will inherit the wealth of Crofts ltd and his father's status. *They represent not just the ruling classes, but also the rich who control and own all major industry in the country.*

Gerald, however, is slightly different. Although Eric agrees with The Inspector, that workers ought to be able to strike, "we try for higher profits, why shouldn't they try for higher wages", Gerald disagrees. ***Because he so passionately disagrees, Priestley decides it should be Gerald who exposes The Inspector as a fake***. Gerald takes command, and begins behaving as "though nothing has happened". In this way, Priestley questions whether the younger generation will actually turn out like Gerald, rather than like Sheila and Eric.

(When you read the rest of the essay, notice for yourself how it keeps trying to do each of those 4 things. The most influential place to do these again is in the conclusion, where you always deal with the author's final purpose).

AO2 Analyse the language, form and structure using the correct terminology

The indicative comment might then refer to Mr and Mrs Birling's reactions to The Inspector.

Mr and Mrs Birling of course have a vested interest in keeping the status quo. Birling wants as much profit as possible. This is even part of the attraction in marrying Sheila to Gerald. This is why Birling proposes to bring Crofts ltd and his own business into a financial "alliance" through the marriage. This is also why Mrs Birling suggests to Sheila that she should not condemn Gerald for his possible infidelity, but instead should expect "men of business" to have affairs. Wealth and status are more important than their children.

Mrs Birling's love of status makes her refuse charity to Eva, and Priestley presents this as the final cruelty which drives Eva to suicide. Although this apparently leads to the death of Mrs Birling's grandchild, she is unrepentant, and refuses to admit that she did "anything wrong". For her the class barriers are too great, and "girls of that class" will never be entitled to her sympathy or understanding.

Although Birling is convinced by The Inspector initially, saying "I would give thousands, yes thousands", he only appears to differ from his wife. Once Gerald has convinced him it was all "a hoax", he now ridicules his own children, "the famous younger generation" who "can't take a joke", through which Priestley symbolises the apparently huge distance between the Birling parents and children.

The indicative content might then refer to the difference between Eric and Sheila and the Birlings, at the end of the play.

In contrast, Eric and Sheila both reject their parents' views, stating that they will "always remember/never forget" The Inspector's teaching. Eric believes, "We did her in all right." Sheila is actually scared of the consequences of her parents' refusal to learn, "And it frightens me the way you talk." This includes Gerald, so she decides to break off her engagement with him, even though in this patriarchal society she will not find a better economic match, saying it is "too soon" to accept Gerald back.

The indicative content might then want to contrast Sheila and Eric with the other young character, Gerald.

Gerald, however, feels little guilt. The Inspector actually complimented him on treating Eva, as Daisy, decently, as he "made her happy for a time". He is now so confident in his own rightness that he asks Sheila to take back the engagement ring immediately. There is also a slight suspicion that Sheila may well accept it in future – Priestley does not give her an outright refusal. This causes us to wonder if The Inspector's lesson, though fully learned, will be retained by the younger generation in the years to come.

The indicative comment might want you to chart the change in Eric and Sheila from the start of the play, possibly including their selfishness and irresponsibility.

So, by the end of the play we have seen Sheila move from vanity, getting Eva sacked because she was "pretty" and better "suited" than Sheila to the dress she wanted to buy, to social responsibility, realising that instead she and her class should look after the girls in "their back rooms counting their pennies". Eric is presented as an alcoholic at the beginning of the play, and has been stealing from his father's business. But by the end of the play he is determined to create a fairer society. His change is perhaps the most radical, as he is the only character who has actually committed a crime.

The indicative comment might then want you to compare the Birlings at the start of the play, possibly including their arrogance.

Although Birling still has the same arrogance he had at the beginning of the play, stating that a man "has to look after his own business and family", he is left exposed by the final phone call, suggesting that a girl has in fact died. The audience will remember The Inspector's last words, that they will "learn a lesson in fire and blood and anguish", which will be the impending tragedy of The First World War and, to his audience, the repeated tragedy of The Second World War.

AO3 Understand the relationships between texts and the contexts in which they were written.

The indicative content will want you to think about context with these key words and ideas:

1. **Social responsibility**
2. **Social change**

3. Societal attitudes
4. Hope for the future

(This is why I teach all my students that they must always write about society at the time the author was writing, and relate that to the author's view of that society – this applies to every single text they ever study!)

Priestley's contemporary audience would also have lived through The Second World War. It is here that Priestley is most subtle in his exploration of the younger generation. Here he is suggesting that society did not really change between the wars. In other words, Eric is very likely to have fallen under the influence of his father. Sheila is very likely to have accepted Gerald's offer of marriage. The arrogance displayed by Birling, that there "will never be war with Germany", is the same arrogance that leads the country into The Second World War. Just as the Birlings refused to learn the lessons of the first death of Eva, the second telephone call and death is a metaphor for The Second World War – those in power in British society refused to learn the lessons they were taught, just as the Birlings refused to learn The Inspector's lessons.

But, his 1945 audience will be filled with adults in their fifties, the Geralds, Erics and Sheilas who still have a chance to change society to make it more socialist. But equally as important, by focusing on "the famous younger generation" Priestley is also directly addressing the younger generation who have just fought the war. They now can learn that "we are all of one body". History shows that "the younger generation" won the day, and 1945 saw a landslide victory for the Labour Party.

What Does it Look Like as an Essay?
How Does Priestley Show the Conflict Between the Younger and Older Generations?

If the Inspector's voice and views are a proxy for Priestley's socialist message, that "we are all one body" and "responsible for each other", then the younger generation are a proxy for his audience in 1945.

Sheila is the most impressed by The Inspector, and he remarks that "we often do (make an impression) on the young ones". She observes that "he inspected us alright" and welcomes his teaching, that we must look after everyone, all the "John Smiths and Eva Smiths", symbolising the working classes.

Priestley creates these characters, not just because they are young, but also because they will have most power in this capitalist society. Sheila and Eric will inherit the Birlings' wealth and status, and Gerald will inherit the wealth of Crofts ltd and his father's status. They represent not just the ruling classes, but also the rich who control and own all major industry in the country.

Gerald, however, is slightly different. Although Eric agrees with The Inspector, that workers ought to be able to strike, "we try for higher profits, why shouldn't they try for higher wages", Gerald disagrees. Because he so passionately disagrees, Priestley decides it should be Gerald who exposes The Inspector as a fake. Gerald takes command, and begins behaving as "though nothing has happened". In this way, Priestley questions whether the younger generation will actually turn out like Gerald, rather than like Sheila and Eric.

Mr and Mrs Birling of course have a vested interest in keeping the status quo. Birling wants as much profit as possible. This is even part of the attraction in marrying Sheila to Gerald. This is why Birling proposes to bring Crofts ltd and his own business into a financial "alliance" through the marriage. This is also why Mrs Birling suggests to Sheila that she should not condemn Gerald for his possible infidelity, but instead should expect "men of business" to have affairs. Wealth and status are more important than their children.

Mrs Birling's love of status makes her refuse charity to Eva, and Priestley presents this as the final cruelty which drives Eva to suicide. Although this apparently leads to the death of Mrs Birling's grandchild, she is unrepentant, and refuses to admit that she did "anything wrong". For her the class barriers are too great, and "girls of that class" will never be entitled to her sympathy or understanding.

Although Birling is convinced by The Inspector initially, saying "I would give thousands, yes thousands", he only appears to differ from his wife. Once Gerald has convinced him it was all "a hoax", he now ridicules his own children, "the famous younger generation" who "can't take a joke", through which Priestley symbolises the apparently huge distance between the Birling parents and children.

In contrast, Eric and Sheila both reject their parents' views, stating that they will "always remember/never forget" The Inspector's teaching. Eric believes, "We did her in all right." Sheila is actually scared of the consequences of her parents' refusal to learn, "And it frightens me the way you talk." This includes Gerald, so she decides to break off her engagement with him, even though in this patriarchal society she will not find a better economic match, saying it is "too soon" to accept Gerald back.

Gerald, however, feels little guilt. The Inspector actually complimented him on treating Eva, as Daisy, decently, as he "made her happy for a time". Now he is now so confident in his own rightness that he asks Sheila to take back the engagement ring immediately. There is also a slight suspicion that Sheila may well accept it in future – Priestley does not give her an outright refusal. This causes us to wonder if The Inspector's lesson, though fully learned, will be retained by the younger generation in the years to come.

So, by the end of the play we have seen Sheila move from vanity, getting Eva sacked because she was "pretty" and better "suited" than Sheila to the dress she wanted to buy, to social responsibility, realising that instead she and her class should look after the girls in "their back rooms counting their pennies". Eric is presented as an alcoholic at the beginning of the play, and has been stealing from his father's business. But by the end of the play he is determined to create a fairer society. His change is perhaps the most radical, as he is the only character who has actually committed a crime.

Although Birling still has the same arrogance he had at the beginning of the play, stating that a man "has to look after his own business and family", he is left exposed by the final phone call, suggesting that a girl has in fact died. The audience will remember The Inspector's last words, that they will "learn a lesson in fire and blood and anguish", which will be the impending tragedy of The First World War and, to his audience, the repeated tragedy of The Second World War.

Priestley's contemporary audience would also have lived through The Second World War. It is here that Priestley is most subtle in his exploration of the younger generation. Here he is suggesting that society did not really change between the wars. In other words, Eric is very likely to have fallen under the influence of his father. Sheila is very likely to have accepted Gerald's offer of marriage. The arrogance displayed by Birling, that there "will never be war with Germany", is the same arrogance that leads the country into The Second World War. Just as the Birlings refused to learn the lessons of the first death of Eva, the second telephone call and death is a metaphor for The Second World War – those in power in British society refused to learn the lessons they were taught, just as the Birlings refused to learn The Inspector's lessons.

But, his 1945 audience will be filled with adults in their fifties, the Geralds, Erics and Sheilas who still have a chance to change society to make it more socialist. But equally as important, by focusing on "the famous younger generation" Priestley is also directly addressing the younger generation who have just fought the war. They now can learn that "we are all of one body". History shows that "the younger generation" won the day, and 1945 saw a landslide victory for the Labour Party.

This is 1062 words.

Many of my students, who are not in a top set, are able to write this much. How? Practice, practice, practice. And also belief: "If I work hard, I will keep getting better." Last year, two of my class achieved a grade 8, and one a grade 9 for literature, and there were 62 students in sets above them. It wasn't just that they followed my advice. They chose to work hard, memorising the ideas, testing them with their own ideas and writing without taking a break.

The only research that has been done on English exam answers says that in a 40-45 minute question, students at A*, as it was then, wrote on average 700 words in an essay. This must be your minimum target. You'll probably miss it. So practise. 700 words for grades 8 and 9.

So here is a shorter version of the essay for you:
(Let's pause a minute before you read it. This essay above will get you full marks because of the ideas in it. However, it is not written in a perfect order, because I wrote it just using the indicative content from the mark scheme, which goes in this order: AO1, AO2, AO3. That's the way you should revise for essay writing. My shorter essay will actually be better because I can redraft it to deal with points in a more natural order. That's what you should do next if you can't write 1000 words in the exam).

Short Essay

The Inspector's voice and views are a **proxy** for *Priestley's socialist message*, that "we are all one body" and "responsible for each other". Sheila and Eric are made to learn this lesson, that we must look after everyone, all the "John Smiths and Eva Smiths", **symbolising** *the working classes.*

Priestley **creates** these young **characters** in *1912* because they will have most power in this capitalist society through their inheritance of wealth and status. They **represent** *the ruling classes of 1945.*

Although Eric shares *socialist views*, "we try for higher profits, why shouldn't they try for higher wages", Gerald disagrees and Priestley makes Gerald behave as "though nothing has happened". Therefore, Priestley **questions** *whether the younger generation will actually turn out like* Gerald, rather than like Sheila and Eric.

Like Gerald, Birling *worships profit*. He even describes Sheila's marriage to Gerald *as a business "alliance"*. This is also why Mrs Birling suggests Sheila should accept Gerald's infidelity and should expect "men of business" to have affairs. *Wealth and status are more important than their children, so capitalism destroys their humanity.*

Priestley **shows** Mrs Birling's lack of humanity is caused by her love of status. Although denying charity to Eva, and apparently losing her grandchild, she refuses to admit she did "anything wrong". For her the *class barriers* are too great, and "girls of that class" will never be entitled to her sympathy or understanding.

In contrast, Birling appears to repent: "I would give thousands, yes thousands". However, once Gerald convinces him it was all "a hoax", he ridicules his own children, "the famous younger generation" who "can't take a joke". Priestley **symbolises** the apparently huge distance between the Birling parents and children.

In contrast, Eric and Sheila both reject their parents' views, and will "always remember" The Inspector's teaching. Eric believes, "We did her in all right."   Sheila is scared of the consequences of their refusal to learn, "And it frightens me." Consequently, she ends her engagement, saying it is "too soon" to accept Gerald, even though she will not find a better economic match *in this* **patriarchal society**.

Gerald, however, feels little guilt, as The Inspector judged he "made her happy for a time". He arrogantly asks Sheila to take back the engagement ring. Surprisingly, Priestley doesn't make her refuse. *This causes us to wonder if The Inspector's lesson, though fully learned, will be retained by the younger generation in the years to come.*

We have seen Sheila **move from** vanity, getting Eva sacked because she was "pretty", *to social responsibility, sympathising with working class girls* "counting their pennies". Eric **shifts from** an alcoholic abuser, stealing from his father's business, to being determined to *create a fairer society*: "I agree with Sheila."

In contrast, Birling's arrogant belief that a man "has to look after his own business and family", **doesn't change**, *which summons the final phone call and a second death*. The **audience** will remember The Inspector's last words, that they will "learn a lesson in fire and blood and anguish", *reminding them that this capitalist **viewpoint** led to the **tragedies** of both world wars*.

Thus Priestley subtly **portrays** the younger generation, ***suggesting society*** *did not **change*** *between the wars. After 1912, Eric was probably influenced by his father. Sheila probably accepted Gerald's offer of marriage. Birling's arrogance, **represented** by believing we "will never be war with Germany", leads to World War Two. The refusal to learn the lessons of Eva's death, leads to the second death, which is a **metaphor** for The Second World War. They are a **symbol** of the **ruling classes'** refusal to learn from war and social unrest.*

But, *Priestley's **contemporary audience** is filled with adults in their fifties, the Geralds, Erics and Sheilas who can create a socialist society.* **Priestley also directly addresses** *the "younger generation" who have just fought the war*, teaching "we are all of one body". *History shows this "younger generation" created a socialist **future**, with Labour's landslide victory in 1945.*

659 words

- The words in bold are subject terminology.
- The words in italics are where I keep explaining Priestley's purpose, using context like an embedded quotation.

What, why didn't you make it 700 words?
I spent just as long editing this essay as I did writing it. If I can make it this short now, I can write less expertly in the exam, where under pressure I will write more words to make the same points.

But I also train myself to be a much better writer, something that will repay me again and again, for the whole of my life. Sure, it will also make it much easier for me to get top grades at GCSE, but that's a tiny benefit compared to the next 70 years, isn't it? That's why I teach anyway. I hope it works for you.

What does the AQA mark scheme say?
1. Convincing
2. Critical analysis
3. Conceptualised
4. Exploration of context to author's and contemporary readers' perspectives
5. Give interpretation(s)
6. Response to the whole text
7. Analyse it as a play, and deal with the structure
8. Precise references
9. Analysis of writer's methods
10. Subject terminology used judiciously

11. Exploration of effects of writer's methods on reader

They basically mean this:

What you must do
1. Give more than one interpretation of the characters or events.
2. Make sure you write about Priestley's viewpoint and ideas about his society at the time, in 1945
3. Write about how the society of 1945 would respond to these ideas, characters and events.
4. Write about the ending of the play, to show how characters have or haven't changed
5. Write about the ending to show Priestley's viewpoint.

When you do it, make sure you
1. Embed quotations all the time
2. Only use terminology if it helps explain an idea*

*You will notice that I have not named any verbs, adjectives, nouns, adverbs, because that is just dumb. Naming parts of the sentence tells you nothing about the ideas in it, so the examiner realises you are just sticking this in to use terminology, but it is not "judicious". Your teacher may think that the examiner wants this anyway. If so, ask them what would have happened if they had used terminology in this way in their degree.

Better still, go back and look at the words in bold in the short essay. This is subject terminology.

What does "subject terminology" mean?
The words a student of literature at university would use in *nearly every* literature essay. You could argue that connectives fall under this category as well, if you want.

What does the Edexcel mark scheme say?

1. There is an assured personal response
2. Discerning choice of references to the text
3. You write in a critical style
4. You have perceptive interpretations
5. The understanding of relevant contexts is excellent (so, Priestley's context, and the different one of his audience).
6. Context is integrated convincingly into the response (like an embedded quotation)

An Inspector Calls – An Essay on Social Class

Written by viewer Ipthi Chowdhury, and printed with his kind permission. Thanks Ipthi!

(This essay scored 30/30)

Priestley explores the concept of social class as well as its implementation as a regrettable feature of the early 1900s. Edwardian commitment to social class forms a key aspect of society, which Priestley attempts to challenge. The importance of social class is presented through its impact.

- *Level 3 A03 Because is it general and not related to the meaning of the play yet. This means it is only showing 'some understanding'.*
- *It also shows you how the examiner is trying to make up their mind as early as possible in your answer.*

In An Inspector Calls, social class is presented as a capitalist and exploitative system. Priestley conveys this reality through Mrs Birling, who attacks Eva Smith's character in a prejudicial manner.

- *Level 4 A01 – the examiner now feels this is a clear explanation and reference, but it isn't linked to a quotation yet, so isn't really offering a "thoughtful" or "developed" interpretation.*

She describes her as being from "girls of that class ". Immediately, Priestley evokes the audience's anger through the use of the pronoun "that": linguistically, revealing the connotations of derogatory feelings on the basis of social status.

- *Level 5 A01 – Notice how he goes up a level as soon as he links his interpretation to a quotation. It shows "apt references integrated into interpretation", because it is an integrated quotation, embedded in the sentence. Notice that naming "that" as a pronoun earns Ipthi nothing for subject terminology, in AO2 – you don't have to name the parts of speech. In fact, doing so sounds a bit clumsy.*

This would be condemned by the contemporary audience, given the recent war effort in 1945, where the nation united regardless of background, in order to defend Britain.

- *Level 5 A03 – notice that Ipthi relates this bit of context to the meaning, an attack on capitalism, and to the 'contemporary' audience. Context on its own, as we saw in the introduction, scores low marks.*

Priestley highlights the exploitative element through Gerald's admission, "I didn't feel about her as she felt about me". The theme of upper-class selfishness is recalled here evidently, since Gerald's keeping of Eva Smith as a "mistress" implies he used her, and sexually exploited her, having played with her feelings.

Moreover, Priestley maintains Gerald's **character** as constant, giving his later comments that "everything is fine now". The **irony depicts** the upper-class as callous and uncouth, further **inviting the audience** to **dissociate** from **the social system**.

- *Level 5 A02. So the first reward for terminology is graded "examination of writer's methods with subject terminology used effectively to support". I've placed the 'terminology' in bold. 'Terminology' means the vocabulary you would need to use when writing about ANY literary text.*

Priestley expresses the emphasis on social class as a capitalistic trait, that isn't socially cooperative. This is notable when Mr Birling discusses his business ethics: "it's my duty to keep labour costs down. Our labour costs". Here, Priestley presents Mr Birling as a direct antithesis to social reformation. The possessive pronouns "my" and "our" carry connotations of selfishness and greed, elements Priestley considers to be inherently representative of the nature of capitalism.

Contextually, Priestley evokes the audience's dissatisfaction towards Mr Birling's words. Atlee's newly elected Labour government made increasing social welfare a manifesto commitment in 1945. Mr Birling's business interests would be deemed as counter-productive, following an ideology of extreme austerity. In this way Priestley establishes social class firmly as part of the capitalist economic agenda in the play.

- *Level 6 A01 – the examiner is impressed with this detailed analysis of the use of single words in the quotation. Here it is worth calling them by their parts of speech, because Priestley is using them to emphasise possession, and doing it more than once.*
- *Level 6 A03 – here Ipthi directly relates the context to the meaning of play and Priestley's purpose is persuading his audience to vote Labour.*
- *It's also worth asking if you could memorise the two paragraphs above, and use them in any essay on the play. I think you can, and you will have a level 6 section to your essay, come what may.*

Attitudes towards **social class** are **presented** by Priestley as evolving and important. Priestley **appears** to credit the rise of socialism for the fall of **class hierarchies**, through the younger generation of **characters**. Eric's **development** from being "half assertive" and "half shy", to challenging his father's business **ethics**: "why shouldn't they ask for higher wages?" marks his renouncement of upper-class traditionalism and his adoption of a more **morally** considerate socialism.

- *Level 6 A02 – again I have highlighted the terminology which you would use to write about ANY literature text. There are other words which are specific to An Inspector Calls, like 'socialism' etc.*

The question appears as an open challenge to his father and highlights his maturity. However, through Eric **as a construct**, Priestley presents capitalism to his audience as having an illogical and unfair fallacy. Eric's question would have been deemed as reasonable and raise ethical concerns.

- *Level 6 AO2 – I've highlighted 'construct' because it the one word every examiner is drawn to – it is the one which shows you are aware everything in the text is there for a reason, linked to the author's attempt to influence how we think. ALWAYS use it.*

Likewise, Sheila is employed as a construct to challenge upper-class exploitation with a moral argument that, "these girls aren't cheap labour – they're people". The adjective "cheap" further highlights the deplorable upper-class perspective of the lower classes. Priestley's construction of Eric and Sheila as corrigible* attempts to educate the audience that social class is outdated and isn't fit for modern times.
By drawing upon the moral failure of the social class system, Priestley generates odium for it.

*capable of being corrected

- *Again, could you memorise the last two paragraphs and use them to end any essay on the play? I think you could. That's 4 level 6 paragraphs, which will propel your essay leaping over grade boundaries.*
- *All Level 6.*

Here it is as one essay:

An Inspector Calls – An Essay on Social Class
Written by viewer Ipthi Chowdhury, and printed with his kind permission. Thanks Ipthi!

(This essay scored 30/30 in only 542 words!)

Priestley explores the concept of social class as well as its implementation as a regrettable feature of the early 1900s. Edwardian commitment to social class forms a key aspect of society, which Priestley attempts to challenge. The importance of social class is presented through its impact.

In An Inspector Calls, social class is presented as a capitalist and exploitative system. Priestley conveys this reality through Mrs Birling, who attacks Eva Smith's character in a prejudicial manner.

She describes her as being from "girls of that class". Immediately, Priestley evokes the audience's anger through the use of the pronoun "that": linguistically, revealing the connotations of derogatory feelings on the basis of social status.

This would be condemned by the contemporary audience, given the recent war effort in 1945, where the nation united regardless of background, in order to defend Britain.

Priestley highlights the exploitative element through Gerald's admission, "I didn't feel about her as she felt about me". The theme of upper-class selfishness is recalled here evidently, since Gerald's keeping of Eva Smith as a "mistress" implies he used her, and sexually exploited her, having played with her feelings.

Moreover, Priestley maintains Gerald's **character** as constant, giving his later comments that "everything is fine now". The **irony depicts** the upper-class as callous and uncouth, further **inviting the audience** to **dissociate** from **the social system**.

Priestley expresses the emphasis on social class as a capitalistic trait, that isn't socially cooperative. This is notable when Mr Birling discusses his business ethics: "it's my duty to keep labour costs down. Our labour costs". Here, Priestley presents Mr Birling as a direct antithesis to social reformation. The possessive pronouns "my" and "our" carry connotations of selfishness and greed, elements Priestley considers to be inherently representative of the nature of capitalism.

Contextually, Priestley evokes the audience's dissatisfaction towards Mr Birling's words. Atlee's newly elected Labour government made increasing social welfare a manifesto commitment in 1945. Mr Birling's business interests would be deemed as counter-productive, following an ideology of extreme austerity. In this way Priestley establishes social class firmly as part of the capitalist economic agenda in the play.

Attitudes towards **social class** are **presented** by Priestley as evolving and important. Priestley **appears** to credit the rise of socialism for the fall of **class hierarchies**, through the younger generation of **characters**. Eric's **development** from being "half assertive" and "half shy", to challenging his father's business **ethics**: "why shouldn't they ask for higher wages?" marks his renouncement of upper-class traditionalism and his adoption of a more **morally** considerate socialism.

The question appears as an open challenge to his father and highlights his maturity. However, through Eric **as a construct**, Priestley presents capitalism to his audience as having an illogical and unfair fallacy. Eric's question would have been deemed as reasonable and raise ethical concerns.

Likewise, Sheila is employed as a construct to challenge upper-class exploitation with a moral argument that, "these girls aren't cheap labour – they're people". The adjective "cheap" further highlights the deplorable upper-class perspective of the lower classes. Priestley's construction of Eric and Sheila as corrigible* attempts to educate the audience that social class is outdated and isn't fit for modern times.
By drawing upon the moral failure of the social class system, Priestley generates odium for it.

*capable of being corrected

Printed in Great Britain
by Amazon

41156595R00071

The Aviation Noteboo

McDonnell Douglas F-4

PHANTOM

Stewart Wilson

Airlife
England

Contents

Copyright © 2000 Stewart Wilson and Wilson Media Pty Ltd
First published in the UK in 2000
by Airlife Publishing Ltd

First published in Australia by Wilson Media Pty Ltd

British Library Cataloguing-in-Publication Data
A catalogue record for this book is available from the British Library

ISBN 1 84037 216 8

Production and design: Gayla Wilson and Wendy Wilson,
Special thanks to Australian Aviation. Colour profiles by Juanita Franzi.

Printed in Australia

Front cover: USAF Tactical Air Command F-4C Phantom 64-0690.
Frontpiece: A temporary commemorative colour scheme for F-4E 77-0290 in March 1978,
the 5,000th Phantom built by McDonnell at St Louis. It was subsequently delivered to Turkey.

Airlife Publishing Ltd
101 Longden Road, Shrewsbury, SY3 9EB, England
E-mail: airlife@airlifebooks.com
Website: www.airlifebooks.com

Background To Brilliance

When one of the great aviation writers describes an aircraft as "the greatest fighter of the postwar era", it is worth taking note. The fighter to which Bill Gunston was referring is the McDonnell Douglas F-4 Phantom II, a genuine multi role combat aircraft which was developed as a carrier borne naval aircraft and not only served with the USA's maritime air arms - the Navy and Marine Corps - but also with the US Air Force which discovered that in the Phantom, the USAF's nautical 'rivals' had an aircraft superior to anything it could muster.

The result was the first ever purchase of a US Navy fighter by the USAF, in large quantities for firmly land based operations. Of the more than 3,900 Phantoms built for the US services, over 2,600 or two-thirds went to the Air Force.

Eleven other nations also discovered the usefulness of the tough, reliable, superbly performing Phantom. South Korea, Israel, Iran, West Germany, Spain, Greece, Turkey, Japan, Saudi Arabia and Australia all obtained standard or minor variants of standard models, while a re-engined and largely redesigned version was built for the British Royal Navy and Royal Air Force. The only Phantoms not manufactured at McDonnell's St Louis plant were 138 F-4EJs for Japan, these built by Mitsubishi under licence.

The first Phantom flew in May 1958 and the 5,057th and last St Louis built example was handed over in October 1979. The last Japanese Phantom was delivered in May 1981. In the meantime, the Phantom was produced in numerous variations capable of fulfilling a multitude of fighter, bomber, strike, reconnaissance and electronic warfare roles.

Even as the 21st century dawns, the Phantom is still regarded as a front line type in many parts of the world and after upgrades, some will most likely still be serving for at least a decade into the third millennium.

The Phantom has been successfully deployed in several wars during its operational career - Vietnam, the Middle East, the Gulf - and human nature being what it is, "the greatest fighter of the modern era" will probably earn one or two more glories before it is finally put to pasture.

Humble Beginnings

When the McDonnell Aircraft Company of St Louis, Missouri, began development of what would become the Phantom II, it was, in the overall scheme of things, a relatively small organisation without the long traditions of companies like Lockheed, Grumman, Curtiss and Douglas, with which it would merge in 1967 to form the McDonnell Douglas Corporation, now part of the Boeing empire.

Formed in July 1939 by James S McDonnell (or perhaps inevitably, simply 'Mac', as he was universally known), the company in its earliest days had a staff of just two (McDonnell and a secretary) and a tiny rented office next to St Louis Municipal Airport, or Lambert Field.

McDonnell's earliest dabble in aircraft design was in 1928 when he produced the Doodlebug, a two seat light aircraft which was entered in the Guggenheim contest for a 'safe' aircraft. Revolutionary in many ways, the Doodlebug's prospects were killed off by the Great Depression, and McDonnell went to work for other aircraft manufacturers, learning the skills which would later allow him to establish his own organisation.

The re-established McDonnell Aircraft Corporation received its first contract for an aircraft of its own design in September 1941 when the USAAF ordered a prototype of the XP-67 twin engined fighter. This extraordinary looking aircraft featured smooth, contoured 'blended' shapes in order to reduce drag, the very heavy armament of six 37mm cannon and experimental powerplants, two Continental XIV-1430-17/90 water cooled inverted V12s of 1,600hp (1,193kW) each in very tight cowlings.

The XP-67 flew in January 1944 but was plagued by problems with its powerplants and that, in combination with the fact that its intended role - as a bomber destroyer - was redundant by late 1944, meant the project was cancelled after the completion of just one prototype.

The company had not been idle in the meantime, however. In January 1943 it had received an order for its first jet aircraft from the US Navy - the first Phantom. The first of two XFD-1 Phantom prototypes flew in January 1945 and two months later orders were placed for production aircraft under the new designation FH-1. Sixty examples were delivered to the US Navy and the type made history in July 1946 when it became the first American jet aircraft to land on an aircraft carrier, the USS *Franklin D Roosevelt*. The FH-1 was a conventional straight wing single seat fighter powered by two 1,600lb (7.1kN) thrust Westinghouse J30 turbojets and capable of a top speed of 505mph (812km/h).

Modest though the Phantom's success was, it did establish the McDonnell company and allowed it to earn a good reputation with the US military. Several successful (and the odd unsuccessful) designs followed in the late 1940s and early 1950s including the F2H Banshee naval fighter (first flight 1947, 892 built), the experimental XF-88 twin jet long range fighter of 1949 which

Ready to launch. An F-4B of VF-121 'Pacemakers', the Phantom training unit for the USN Pacific Fleet from delivery of its first F4H-1 in late December 1960 to September 1980.

grew into the supersonic F-101 Voodoo for the USAF (1954-1961, 802 built), the F3H Demon naval fighter (1951-1959, 519 built) and the extraordinary XF-85 Goblin experimental 'parasite' fighter of 1948, a tiny jet designed to be carried in the bomb bay of a Convair B-36 bomber and launched when its parent came under threat from enemy aircraft. Afterwards, the Goblin was retrieved by the B-36.

The Demon and the Voodoo, in particular, established McDonnell as an innovative designer and reliable supplier to the US services. Both aircraft incorporated a high degree of technology for their era and featured aerodynamic and structural innovation which enhanced the company's reputation.

It therefore came as something of a disappointment to McDonnell in 1953 when Chance Vought was announced the winner of the competition to supply the US Navy with its first supersonic fighter. Vought's winning design was the F8U Crusader.

Towards Phantom II

Undaunted, and unwilling to lose the momentum it had built up with the Demon and Voodoo, McDonnell pressed on with a new naval strike fighter design without official support. Like so many inspired aircraft designs, the Phantom began life as a private venture without a customer underwriting its early development.

McDonnell called the new aircraft the F3H-G/H Phantom II, and its original design resulted from the company pestering just about anyone connected with the US Navy as to what the service's next generation fighter might be required to be. Questionnaires were left with senior and not so senior Navy officers, people were talked to and listened to and others were invited to visit the factory.

A full size mockup of the new fighter was built in 1954 and appropriate people were invited to inspect it. An aircraft which had a strong family resemblance to its immediate family predecessors was revealed, and one which was also generally similar to the Phantom II as it would eventually appear.

McDonnell family characteristics were evident - such as the jet pipes emerging from the truncated lower rear fuselage with the tail assemblies

The end of the line... the 5,057[th] and last Phantom to emerge from the McDonnell Douglas line at St Louis in October 1979. F-4E 78-0744 was subsequently delivered to South Korea while the last Phantom of all emerged from Mitsubishi's line in Japan in May 1981.

mounted above and behind it on the 'tail cone' - but two major physical characteristics of the definitive Phantom were missing, the anhedral tail-plane and dihedral outer wings. Instead, the F3H-G/H at this early stage had flat wings and horizontal tail surfaces.

The mockup showed a large single seater powered by two afterburning 8,000lb (35.6kN) thrust Wright J65 turbojets (licence built Armstrong Siddeley Sapphires), four 20mm cannon, radar and provision for no fewer than 11 external stores pylons capable of carrying a wide variety of ordnance befitting the aircraft's multi role aspirations. A speed of Mach 1.5 at altitude was promised.

McDonnell's efforts were finally rewarded in November 1954 when the US Navy signed a letter of intent for two aircraft under the designation AH-1, this indicating a primarily attack aircraft rather than a fighter. It should be noted that at the time there was no official requirement for such an aircraft and the move was made as much to keep an innovative design team together as anything else. It turned out to be a wise decision.

The US Navy requested one change to the basic design - replacing the J65s with a pair of the new General Electric J79 turbojets which promised - in its early forms - about 15,000lb (66.7kN) thrust with afterburner. The J79 would find its initial application in the Lockheed F-104 Starfighter, which first flew in 1954.

The incorporation of the larger and considerably more powerful J79s necessitated considerable redesign of the air inlets and ducts. The Phantom was the first fighter to have fully variable inlets, this feature enabling maximum performance to be extracted from the aircraft.

Work on the new fighter rolled on into 1955 but with little purpose as a letter of intent does not constitute a firm order and there was still no official US Navy requirement for the aircraft.

Phantom Finalised

All that changed in the space of an hour in April 1955 when government officials paid a brief visit to the McDonnell factory in St Louis. They brought with them a detailed specification for a fleet defence fighter capable of

The first YF4H-1 Phantom II (BuAer 142259) on the St Louis production line in 1958 in the company of RF-101 Voodoos.

performing a mission hitherto unheard of - a 250nm (465km) radius of action combined with two hours combat air patrol (CAP) on station. In that mission, the Phantom had to detect, intercept and destroy unfriendly aircraft.

The following fortnight saw frenzied activity on the Phantom's design: it became a tandem two seater (pilot and a very necessary fire control officer); it lost its internal guns and replaced them with four Raytheon Sparrow radar guided air-to-air missiles mounted semi-recessed under the wide and flat fuselage bottom; all but the centreline stores hardpoint (for a 600 USgal/ 2,271 litre external fuel tank) were initially eliminated, although eight were reinstated when the multirole possibilities of the aircraft were recognised; internal fuel capacity was increased; the outer wings (which folded) had their chord increased to give the characteristic 'sawtooth' leading edge and 12 degrees of dihedral was applied; the one piece slab 'stabilator' was given firstly 15 degrees and then the definitive 23 degrees anhedral to remove it from the turbulent air created by wing wake at high angles of attack and to counter the rolling effect of the outer wings in yawed flight; and a folding flight refuelling probe was designed for the starboard forward fuselage.

The revisions pleased the US Navy and approval to proceed with the detail and engineering design was given. What emerged was a great advance in fighter-bomber design, although the Phantom's potential was probably not fully appreciated until it took to the air three years later.

Structurally, the new Phantom's wing comprised a one piece centre section and centre wing structure from wing fold to wing fold with the part that passed through the fuselage made up of a torsion box between the front and main spars which was sealed to form two integral fuel tanks. The wing's trailing edge was a one piece aluminium honeycomb structure while the flaps and ailerons were of conventional all metal construction. The trailing edge flaps were hydraulically operated (three independent systems were fitted) as were the 'blown' leading edge flaps and the airbrakes under each wing.

The fuselage was of conventional all metal semi monocoque construction, the undercarriage (stressed for a descent rate of 22ft/sec at 33,000lb) was hydraulically actuated with single main wheels and double nosewheel. Roll control was provided by conventional ailerons plus upper wing spoilers, the wings were swept back at an angle of 45 degrees and the quickly reinstated nine hardpoints (centre fuselage plus four under each wing) were capable of carrying a load of 16,000lb (7,257kg) between them.

The variable engine air intakes and their associated ducting were nothing short of masterpieces of design and the major contributor to the Phantom's exceptional performance. They were designed for optimum pressure recovery over the full operating envelope of the aircraft, each intake constructed so that it did not swallow the moving boundary layer created by the forward fuselage.

This stale air was sheared away by large flat ramps and flow smoothness was assured by suction applied through 12,500 tiny perforations in a movable intake wall section or splitter plate. The movable ramp could be positioned at achieve best pressure recovery in the intake at any Mach number by an automatic system.

If the part of the aeroplane where the air goes in received special attention, so did the bits where the jet efflux leaves the aircraft. The result was not particularly pretty but extremely effective, and this was later proven when the Rolls-Royce Spey powered Phantom for Britain was developed. The Spey turbofans' greater diameters necessitated larger exhausts which upset the previously finely balanced design. The result was that despite considerably more power, Britain's Phantoms were notably slower than their American counterparts.

First Orders - XF4H-1 Phantom

In May 1955, McDonnell was given approval to go ahead with the new design and build two prototypes under the designation XF4H-1. As insurance against the aircraft failing, prototypes of the Chance Vought XF8U-3 Crusader III were also ordered. A new design with little in common with earlier Crusaders (apart from the designation and name), the XF8U-3 was a single engined single seater which carried less than the Phantom, and despite a generally successful test programme, lost the production contract to its McDonnell rival.

Three years after contract to build the prototypes was awarded, the first McDonnell XF4H-1 Phantom II (BuAer serial number 142259) flew from Lambert Field, St Louis on 27 May 1958 in the hands of company test pilot Robert Little and was immediately transferred to Edwards Air Force Base for trials. The second aircraft (142260) first flew in October 1958.

Evaluation trials against the Crusader III were completed by late 1958 and in December of that year McDonnell was awarded a contract covering 23 development (including the first two) and 24 production aircraft. These were originally designated F4H-1, then F4H-1F from March 1961 and finally F-4A when the US armed forces introduced a common aircraft designation system in September 1962. For convenience, we'll refer to the Phantom by its F-4 designations from now on, unless it is necessary to do otherwise. Similarly, although the aircraft's name was strictly 'Phantom II', simply 'Phantom' will be used as there is no chance of confusion with the earlier FH-1 Phantom.

Two views of the first Phantom. A significant era in the history of modern military aviation began on 27 May 1958 with the maiden flight of this aircraft.

F-4A Phantom

Deliveries of the 45 F-4A Phantoms began in December 1960 to US Navy squadrons VF-101 and VF-121 detachments for transitional training. All were powered by J79-GE-2 engines each providing 10,350lb (46.0kW) dry thrust and 16,150lb (71.8kN) with afterburner and were used for test, evaluation and training duties.

The first 21 aircraft were regarded as pre production models and the remainder full production aircraft, although there were many variations in detail specification as improvements and modifications were introduced (and often retrofitted) during production. The last of the batch was delivered on 14 September 1961.

The first 18 aircraft featured the original 'flat' canopy design but from aircraft number 19, the definitive Phantom raised canopy (and seat line) was fitted. Early aircraft were fitted with APQ-50 radar with a 24 inch (60cm) diameter scanner dish, while from number 19 APQ-72 radar with its 32 inch (81cm) diameter dish was fitted, necessitating a larger nose radome. An infra-red seeker was mounted in a small housing under the radome, that and the new canopy resulting in a Phantom which was externally similar to the first major production model, the F-4B.

Other modifications introduced to the F-4A included fitting the larger and definitive inlet splitter plate and associated hinged ramp walls and other features of the highly efficient and complex intake system; additional weapons pylons were incorporated; the leading and trailing edge flaps 'blowing' system was made operative; the retractable flight refuelling probe fitted; and weapons/navigation systems equipment such as the General Electric ASA-32 autopilot and Lear AJB-3 bombing system installed.

Operationally, US Navy squadron VF-74 (the 'Be-devilers') became the first fleet squadron to operate the F-4A in July 1961 and achieved carrier qualification four months later. Some of the F-4As were subsequently converted to full F-4B standards and others (which weren't) redesignated as TF-4A trainers.

The 11th F4H-1/F-4A Phantom undergoing trials in 1961 carrying 22 Mk.83 500lb (227kg) bombs. Note the early radome size, canopy shape and inlet/splitter vane configuration.

World Records

While the Phantom was undergoing its early development and preparation for service, it set about proving its prodigious performance capabilities with a series of world speed, altitude and time to height records. The first of these was set in early December 1959 when Cdr Lawrence Flint, USN, took the second prototype to 98,577ft (30,046m) in a zoom climb (Project *Top Flight*) to set a world absolute altitude record.

No fewer than 12 other class or world records were set by F-4A and F-4B Phantoms between 1960 and 1962, among them: world absolute speed (Project *Skyburner*) 1,606.3mph (2,585.0km/h) or Mach 2.6 in November 1961 (Col Bob Robinson USMC); 500km closed circuit speed 1,216.76mph/1,958.1km/h (September 1960, Lt-Col Thomas Miller USMC); 100km closed circuit speed (in effect a constant 3g turn over a period of 2m 40.9sec in this case) 1,390.24mph/2,237.3km/h (September 1960, Cdr J F Davis USN).

Possibly the most prestigious of all the Phantom's speed records was absolute speed over 3 kilometres at a height not exceeding 100 metres or 328 feet. In an aircraft such as the Phantom, such low altitude antics can only imagined.

The Phantom took the record in August 1961 (Project *Sageburner*) when Lt Huntington Hardisty USN recorded a speed of 902.769mph (1,452.8km/h) or Mach 1.25 - and all at no more than 175 feet (53m) above the ground!

Project *High Jump* covered a series of time to height records set by F-4B Phantoms in 1961-62. Measured from a standing start on the runway, the flights resulted in some impressive figures: to 9,000m (29,527ft) in 61.68sec; to 20,000m (65,617ft) 2min 58.50sec; and to 30,000m (98,425ft) 6 min 11.43sec.

The latter (flown by Lt Cdr Del Nordberg USN) had its peak trajectory exceed 100,000 feet (30,480m), or higher than the absolute altitude record set just over two years previously. The records proved the Phantom's extraordinary performance, but subsequent production models would also prove its efficacy in the combat roles for which it was designed.

Phantom record breaker. The second prototype YF4H-1 Phantom (BuAer 142260) photographed in January 1961. This aircraft was remarkable in that it was responsible for setting both world altitude and speed records.

F-4B Phantom

The first major production Phantom for the US Navy and US Marine Corps, the F-4B, was similar to later F-4As (with APQ-72 radar, infra red detector and raised canopy) but was powered by two J79-GE-8 engines offering 10,900lb (48.5kN) dry thrust and 17,000lb (75.6kN) with afterburner. Maximum takeoff weight was 54,600lb (24,766kg). The more powerful engines made slightly larger inlets necessary in combination with changed inlet ramp geometry.

The first F-4B (BuAer 148363) flew on 25 March 1961, deliveries to the US Navy began in June 1961 and the first USMC unit to receive the Phantom was VMF-314 in June 1962. The first operational squadron (rather than training unit) to fly the F-4B was VF-74 aboard USS *Forrestal*. The Phantom's combat debut was recorded on 6 August 1964 when F-4Bs from VF-142 and VF-143 operating from USS *Constellation* provided cover for aircraft attacking North Vietnamese torpedo boat bases.

The Phantom's first air-to-air combat victory occurred on 9 April 1965 when Lt T M Murphy and Ens R J Fegan from VF-96 (USS *Ranger)* shot down a Chinese MiG-17, but the F-4B was then itself shot down by another Chinese fighter.

F-4B production amounted to 649 aircraft (including 12 F-4Gs - see below), the final example delivered in January 1967. The 1,000th Phantom

F-4Bs BuAer 148369 (foreground), 150417 (centre) and 148385 (rear) of VF-101 'Grim Reapers' Detachment A, the USN's Atlantic Fleet Training unit for the Phantom.

from the St Louis production line was F-4B BuAer 152276, delivered in July 1965.

The F-4B's primary role was as a fleet defence fighter with secondary ground attack capability, although this capability was substantial with a maximum ordnance load of 16,000lb (7,258kg) available. In the fighter role the armament was four Sparrow III radar homing air-to-air missiles recessed under the fuselage plus two more on wing pylons; or four Sparrows and four Sidewinders.

The electronic equipment fit included a General Electric ASA-32 autopilot, Lear AJB-3 bombing system, Eclipse-Pioneer dead reckoning navigation computer, AiResearch air data computer, Raytheon radio altimeter, ACF infra-red detector and Magnavox APR-27 surface-air missile launch warning receiver.

F-4G: 12 aircraft to the same mechanical standard as the F-4B were produced as the F-4G, incorporating an ASW-21 two way digital data link. This 'G' model should not to be confused with the later F-4G Wild Weasel radar suppression aircraft based on the F-4E. The first of these early F-4Gs (BuAer 15041) was flown on 20 March 1963 and the conversions (performed on the production line) were delivered to the US Marine Corps during the course of the year.

They were used by USMC squadron VF-213 in Vietnam during 1964-65, operating from the USS *Kitty Hawk*. The survivors were rebuilt as standard F-4Bs from 1966, seven of these subsequently undergoing another conversion, this time to F-4Ns.

RF-4B: The RF-4B was a photo-reconnaissance variant for the USMC, using the reconnaissance systems of the USAF's RF-4C housed in its lengthened nose. Forty-six conversions were completed, the first (BuAer 151975) flying on 12 March 1965 with deliveries stretching between May 1965 and December 1970. No dual controls or armament were fitted and the final 12 aircraft had the wider main wheels and 'thick' wing of the F-4J.

DF-4B: Designation applied to some Phantoms modified for use as 'mother' aircraft to remotely piloted vehicles (RPVs) and drones.

EF-4B: This designation was allocated in late 1976 to a handful of F-4Bs which had been serving with US Navy squadron VAQ-33 as fleet electronic warfare support aircraft as high speed targets and threat simulators. Two F-4Js

A major milestone: the 1,000th Phantom, F-4B BuAer 152276 rolled off the line in July 1965. More than 4,000 others were still to come.

performing a similar role were redesignated EF-4Js at the same time. All carried some special items of electronic equipment.

QF-4B: Itself an RPV used for various research, weapons and combat trials. Although controlled from the ground, the 44 Phantoms converted usually flew with a safety pilot on board. The first conversion (BuAer 148365) was flown in 1970.

NF-4B: Two F-4Bs used for various test programmes, the 'N' in the designation signifying the aircraft had undergone structural modifications which would prevent them from being reconverted to an operational standard.

F-4N: A major operational F-4B conversion, the first of 228 (BuAer 153034) flew on 4 June 1972. The idea was to bring older surviving F-4Bs up to a standard similar to that of the F-4J (see below) by rebuilding them (including the incorporation of some new structural parts) and fitting upgraded equipment, systems and avionics.

Included in the upgrade were completely new structural components to extend life by between 3500 and 5000 hours; the fitting of F-4J style slotted stabilators; an upgraded electrical system (including new wiring); and various systems and equipment upgrades including a helmet sight Visual Target Acquisition System (VTAS), Sidewinder Expanded Acquisition Mode (SEAM), Auto Altitude Reporting, dogfight computer, air-to-air Identification Friend or Foe (IFF), and one way data link.

The first F-4N was delivered in February 1973 and the type remained in service with the Marine Corps Reserve into the 1980s.

QF-4N: A remotely controlled target drone conversation of the F-4N with all unnecessary operational equipment removed to save weight. About 60 conversions performed from late 1982.

A busy shipboard scene with F-4B BuAer 153915 of VF-121 'Pacemakers' being tended by the deck crew. As the US Navy Pacific Fleet Phantom training unit, the squadron operated the F-4 for nearly 20 years. 153915 was the last F-4B built, delivered in January 1967. This photo was taken two months later.

The F-4N was a substantial upgrade of the F-4B undertaken from 1972. This one belongs to the USN's VF-111 'Sundowners' squadron, a unit which saw service in Vietnam.

The first of 46 RF-4B reconnaissance versions of the F-4B (BuAer 151975) which first flew in March 1965. The RF-4B's mission equipment was similar to the USAF's RF-4C.

McDONNELL F-4B PHANTOM

Powerplants: Two 10,900lb (48.5kN) dry thrust or 17,000lb (75.6kN) with afterburner General Electric J79-GE-8/8B turbojets. Internal fuel capacity 1,987 USgal (7,522 litres). Max external fuel 1,341 USgal (5076 litres).

Dimensions: 38ft 5in (11.71m); length 58ft 3in (17.75m); height 16ft 5in (5.00m); wing area 530sq ft (49.2m²).

Weights: Loaded 44,600lb (20,230kg); max overload 54,600lb (24,766kg).

Armament: Four or six AIM-7D or 7E Sparrow III semi-active radar homing AAMs or four Sparrows and four AIM-9 Sidewinder infra-red AAMs; max ordnance load 16,000lb (7,258kg) on centreline and four underwing hardpoints.

Performance: Max speed Mach 2.4 (1,375kt/2,550km/h) at 48,000ft (14,630m) or Mach 2.2 (1,260kt/2,334km/h) with missiles; max speed at sea level Mach 1.2 (795kt/I1,473km/h); initial climb (interceptor) 28,000ft (8,534m)/min; low level tactical radius (6,000lb/2,722kg load) 350nm (650km); intercept radius 800nm (1,482km); unrefuelled ferry range 2,000nm (3,705km).

F-4C Phantom

The early success of the Phantom gave the US Air Force little choice but to take a close look at the aircraft. Its investigations led to the unprecedented action of purchasing an aircraft which had been designed for carrier operations.

A series of direct competitive evaluations against existing USAF aircraft - notably the Convair F-106 Delta Dart fighter - was ordered in 1961 under the auspices of Operation Highspeed. The USAF found in the Phantom an aircraft which was superior in most respects to anything it had at the time - better radar than any USAF fighter, better payload/range characteristics than any USAF attack aircraft, better serviceability and less maintenance burden than any USAF supersonic fighter and considerable potential for development. Interestingly, the best USAF serviceability/maintenance record among its supersonic fighters was held by McDonnell's own F-101 Voodoo.

Other F-4Bs were loaned to the USAF in 1962 for further evaluation and in March of that year the aircraft was ordered in large quantities, sufficient to re-equip 16 of its 23 Tactical Air Command Wings as a true multirole fighter-bomber.

The USAF's first Phantom model was initially designated the F-110A but this was quickly changed to F-4C as part of a general realignment of USAF/ USN designations. Externally similar to the Navy's F-4B, the C was intended as a 'minimum change' variant which retained folding wings and an arrester hook, as did all subsequent versions intended for shore based operations.

Nevertheless, there were some important changes - the addition of a cartridge/pneumatic starting system instead of the Navy's method which required an external hose connection; the replacement of the flight refuelling probe designed for the Navy's probe and drogue system with a receptacle on the top of the fuselage behind the canopy for the USAF's 'flying boom' system; the fitting of larger and lower pressure tyres offering better footprint characteristics and allowing the installation of bigger, anti skid brakes (slight bulges were placed in the wing roots to accommodate them); more complete dual controls in the rear cockpit (at first, both USAF Phantom crewmembers were pilots); the rear instrument panel was lower for a better view; and various items of equipment were modified or upgraded. The 'two pilots' policy was abandoned in 1969, the rear cockpit controls removed and the backseater became a 'Wizzo' - Weapons Systems Officer.

The F-4C's avionics were different to its predecessors' and included APQ-100 radar with enhanced ground mapping capability for bombing missions, a Litton ASN-48 inertial navigation system and an AJB-7 all altitude nuclear bombing

The F-4C Phantom was the first version for the USAF, initial deliveries taking place in November 1963. Production amounted to 583 F-4Cs with the last one delivered in May 1966. This is 63-7672 of the 114th Tactical Fighter Training Squadron, Oregon ANG, a late user of the F-4C between 1984 and 1989.

system. Power was provided by J79-GE-15 engines which gave the same power as the F-4B's -8s but had minor modifications including those necessary for the self contained cartridge/pneumatic starting system.

Commensurate with the F-4C's multirole future with the USAF, it was capable of carrying all of the force's tactical stores including the GAM-83B (later AGM-12) Bullpup air-ground missile and the Mk.28 'special' (nuclear) weapon. A gun pod housing a General Electric M61A1 20mm six barrel rotary cannon with 1,200 rounds could be placed on the centreline stores pylon. AIM-7D/E Sparrow radar homing, AIM-9 Sidewinder heat seeking and AIM-4D Falcon heat seeking missiles made up the air-to-air component.

The first production F-4C (62-12199) flew on 27 May 1963, deliveries to the 4453rd Combat Crew Training Wing at MacDill AFB Florida began in November 1963 and the first combat unit to receive the aircraft was the 12th

Several F-4Bs flew in USAF colours during 1962 for evaluation purposes. The USAF quickly discovered the many virtues of the new naval fighter and had little choice but to order it. BuAer 149405 is photographed here during the trials.

Tactical Fighter Wing (TFW) in early 1964. Initial operational capability was achieved in October 1964.

The USAF's first two MiG kills of the Vietnam War were recorded on 10 July 1965 when F-4Cs from the 45th Tactical Fighter Squadron despatched a pair of MiG-17s using Sidewinders.

F-4C production ended on 4 May 1966 with the delivery of the 583rd example to Tactical Air Command. Apart from TAC, USAF F-4Cs flew with PACAF, USAFE and from 1972 the Air National Guard. The only export was to Spain, which received 36 second hand aircraft between October 1971 and September 1972.

EF-4C: The designation EF-4C was an informal one applied to 36 F-4Cs converted to Wild Weasel electronic reconnaissance, defence suppression

The first production F-4C (62-12199) at the time of its maiden flight in May 1963.

F-4Cs photographed in early 1966 wearing Vietnam era camouflage. The nearest aircraft is 63-7446.

Bombed up F-4C 63-7656 formates with a KC-135A tanker, the two aircraft essential partners in many operational situations.

and electronic countermeasures (ECM) duties in 1968. Armed with AGM-45 Shrike anti-radiation missiles (and normal weapons), they equipped the 52nd and 67th TFWs at Okinawa and then Thailand on raids into North Vietnam. These were only partially successful due to problems with the Shrike and by 1974 the survivors had reverted to standard F-4C configuration.

RF-4C: At the same time the USAF was initially evaluating the Phantom to re-equip its tactical fighter wings, it also looked at an unarmed tactical reconnaissance variant. The result was an extremely important and long lived new production variant, the RF-4C, ordered in 1963 to replace the McDonnell RF-101C Voodoo.

The first of two YRF-4Cs (converted from F-4Bs 62-12200 and 62-12201) flew on 8 August 1963 and the first production RF 4C (63-7440) on 18 May 1964. It remained in production until the end of 1973 by which time 503 had been built. Externally, later RF-4Cs differed from the earlier models in featuring an aerodynamically refined nose shape.

The RF-4C retained the powerplants and other physical characteristics of the F-4C but featured a nose lengthened by 33 inches (84cm) housing APQ-99 forward looking radar with mapping, terrain avoidance and terrain following modes; and three camera bays capable of accommodating forward oblique, panoramic, vertical and left/right oblique cameras in various combinations including high and low altitude versions. APQ-102 side looking radar was installed in the lower fuselage under the front cockpit.

Most of the remainder of the F-4C's tactical equipment - radar, fire control system and weapons - were removed, providing space for numerous

Early (top) and later (bottom) production RF-4Cs displaying their different nose profiles. 63-7440 was the first production model (first flight May 1964) while the camouflaged 65-0945 was built more than two years later.

items of equipment associated with the tactical reconnaissance role: cameras, radar, infra red/Linescan, various electronic intelligence gathering (ELINT) devices, jammers, electronic countermeasures (ECM) and so on.

The result was an extremely capable tactical reconnaissance aircraft which was able to fly long distance sorties in any weather. The RF-4C was highly regarded well into the 1990s, as its equipment was upgraded over the years to include items such as the enormous G-139 centreline pod with high definition LOROP (long range oblique photography) camera, laser reconnaissance equipment, upgraded APQ-102 radar with high resolution mapping, infrared detecting equipment and laser target designators, the latter used for high resolution thermal imaging.

The RF-4C achieved full operational capability with the 16th Tactical Reconnaissance Squadron in August 1965 and ultimately equipped four Tactical Reconnaissance Wings in Tactical Air Command. It was deployed to South-East Asia, Germany and the United Kingdom and served with the Air National Guard from 1972. Two squadrons were committed to the Vietnam War while the RF-4C also played a part in Operation Desert Fox during the 1991 Gulf War. It was withdrawn from US service in 1995.

RF-4Cs have been supplied to Spain (6) and South Korea (18), the Spanish inventory subsequently increasing to 12. Both countries still operated them in 1999.

McDONNELL F-4C/RF-4C PHANTOM

Powerplants: Two 10,900lb (48.5kN) dry thrust or 17,000lb (75.6kN) with afterburner General Electric J79-GE-15 turbojets. F-4C internal fuel capacity 1,973 USgal (7,469 l). RF-4C - internal fuel capacity 1,890 USgal (7,154 l). Max external fuel 1,341 USgal (5,076 l).

Dimensions: F-4C - wing span 38ft 5in (11.71m); length 58ft 3in (17.75m); height 16ft 5in (5.00m); wing area 530sq ft (49.2m²). RF-4C - length 61ft 0in (18.59m).

Weights: F-4C - empty 29,000lb (13,154kg); typical mission weight (combat air patrol) 53,797lb (24,402kg) or (ground attack) 59,453lb (26,968kg). RF-4C - typical mission weight (max external fuel) 52,823lb (23,960kg).

Armament: F-4C - four or six AIM-7D/E Sparrow III radar homing or four Sparrow III and four AIM-9 Sidewinder heat seeking or AIM 4D Falcon heat seeking air-to-air missiles; max weapons load 13,320lb (6,042kg).

Performance: F-4C (combat air patrol) - max speed Mach 2.07 (1,188kt/2,200km/h) at 40,000ft (12,190m); cruising speed 502kt (930km/h); initial climb 8,210ft (2,502m)/min; service ceiling 33,050ft (10,075m); combat radius (including supersonic dash) 250nm (463km). RF-4C (at typical mission weight) - cruising speed 500kt (926km/h); initial climb 8,700ft (2,650m)/min; radius of action 673nm (1,246km). RF-4C (at combat weight) - max speed Mach 2.10 (1,204kt/2,230km/h); at 40,000ft (12,190m); max rate of climb 44,800ft (13,655m)/min at sea level.

F-4D Phantom

March 1964, and the go ahead is given for the production of a Phantom variant tailored to the needs of the USAF rather than being a relatively simple modification of a naval type, as was the case with the F-4C.

The result was the F-4D Phantom, 825 of which were manufactured between the prototype's first flight on 9 December 1965 (64-0929) and the final delivery in February 1968. Of that total, 32 were delivered to Iran while 18 went to South Korea in 1969 from USAF stocks followed by another 18 in 1975.

Powered by J79-GE-15 engines, the F-4D was based on the F-4C airframe but had a substantially updated equipment/avionics fit which included smaller and lighter (due to being partially solid state) APQ-109 fire control radar with air-ground ranging capability; an improved ASG-22 lead computing gyro gunsight; and ASQ-91 weapons release computer and more capable ASG-63 inertial navigation system (INS).

An upgraded electrical system was included along with the capability to carry a wider range of weapons including all the laser guided ('smart') bombs in the USAF's arsenal at the time and the AGM-65 Maverick air-to-ground and AIM-4 Falcon air-to-air missiles, the latter used for a generally unsuccessful period in Vietnam before being replaced by the venerable Sidewinder.

The F-4D became the mainstay of USAF Phantom operations in Vietnam and eventually replaced the 'C' model in that conflict. Although engaged in air-to-ground operations to a very large extent, it also saw considerable air-to-air action and scored its first 'kill' on 5 June 1967 when the 555th TFS's Maj E T Raspberry and Capt F M Gullick downed a MiG-17 near Hanoi using a Sparrow missile. The USAF's last aerial victory of the war was also claimed by an F-4D when the 4th TFS's Capt P D Howman and Lt L W Kullman scored a MiG-21 on 7 January 1973, also using a Sparrow.

Deliveries of the F-4D began in March 1966 to the 36th TFW at Bitburg in Germany while the first US based unit to receive the aircraft was the 4th TFW at based at Seymour Johnson AFB, North Carolina, in January 1967. Vietnam based units began to be equipped in the first half of 1967, the first of them the 8th TFW commanded by Lt Col Robin Olds, whose personal tally for the conflict was two MiG-17s and two MiG-21s, although all of them were in F-4Cs.

The F-4D's period of manufacture coincided with the peak of Phantom

Loaded with Mk.84 bombs and CBU-58 cluster bombs, F-4Ds from the 390th TFS/ 366th TFW replenish their fuel from a KC-135A during the Vietnam War. The wing flew its Ds from Da Nang between January 1968 and April 1969.

An F-4D of the 111th FIS, Texas Air National Guard, photographed in 1988. The unit converted to F-16s the following year.

production, spurred on by the needs of the war in Vietnam. Of the 5,057 Phantoms built at St Louis, no fewer than 3,037 (or 60 per cent) of them were manufactured in the five year period 1965-69, an average of 607 per annum and including the F-4E from mid 1967.

Annual production for that period was: 1965 - 586; 1966 - 618; 1967 - 759; 1968 - 635; 1969 - 439. Production dropped to 282 in 1970 and averaged about 118 per annum after that.

McDONNELL F-4D PHANTOM

Powerplants: Two 10,900lb (48.5kN) dry thrust or 17,000lb (75.6kN) with afterburner General Electric J79-GE-15 turbojets. Internal fuel capacity 1,890 USgal (7,154 l); max fuel with external tanks 3,231 USgal (12,230 l).

Dimensions: Wing span 38ft 5in (11.71m); length 58ft 3in (17.75m); height 16ft 5in (5.00m); wing area 530sq ft (49.2m²).

Weights: Empty 29,000lb (13,154kg); max loaded 59,000lb (26,762kg).

Armament: Intercept - four AIM-7F Sparrow radar homing and four AIM-9 Sidewinder heat seeking air-to-air missiles. Strike - up to 16,000lb (7,258kg) of external stores typically including (alternatively) 15 1,000lb (454kg) Mk.83, 18 750lb (340kg) M-117 or 24 500lb (227kg) Mk.82 bombs; four AGM-12 Bullpup air-to-ground missiles; or 2.75in (7.0cm) rocket pods.

Performance: Max speed (clean) Mach 2.25 (1,290kt/2,390km/h) at 48,000ft (14,630m), Mach 1.15 (800kt/1,480km/h) at sea level; initial climb (mid weight) 28,000ft (8,534m)/min; low level tactical radius (6,000lb/2,722kg bomb load) 350nm (648km); max ferry range 2,000nm (3,705km) at 500kt (925km/h) at 40,000ft (12,190m).

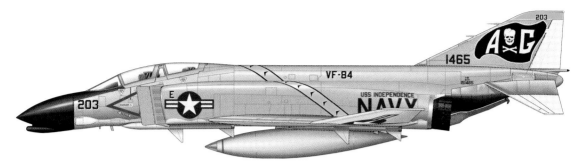

F-4B Phantom BuAer 151465 of VF-84 'Jolly Rogers' squadron, US Navy, aboard USS *Independence* May 1965 at the start of Vietnam tour of duty.

RF-4C Phantom 69-0370 of the 38th TRS, 26th TRW USAF March 1991 during operation 'Desert Storm'; flew 17 reconnaissance missions over Iraq.

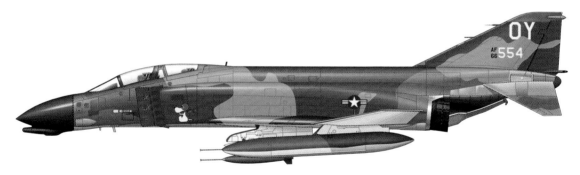

F-4D Phantom 66-7554 of the 555th TFS, 432nd TRW USAF, Thailand July 1971. Although displaying two 'kill' marks, this aircraft in fact downed only one MiG-17 in February 1968.

Not what it seems! This F-4E is actually 67-0270 of the 21st TFTS, 35th TFW USAF, George AFB late 1980s, not 67-6270 as marked, a non existent Phantom serial. This F-4E downed a MiG-21 in July 1972.

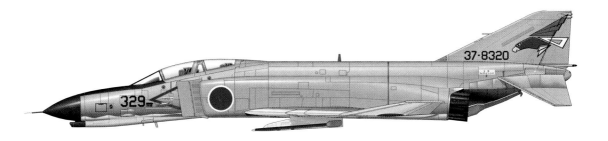

F-4EJ Kai Phantom 37-8320 of the 302nd Hikotai JASDF, 1995.

F-4J Phantom BuAer 153893 of VMFA-312 'Checkerboards' USMC, Beaufort MCAS July 1976. Squadron titling in red, white and blue to celebrate US Bicentenary.

Phantom FG.1 XT859 of 892 Squadron RN Fleet Air Arm aboard HMS *Ark Royal* in 1978. Red, white and blue striping on radome left over from HM The Queen's Silver Jubilee celebration in 1977.

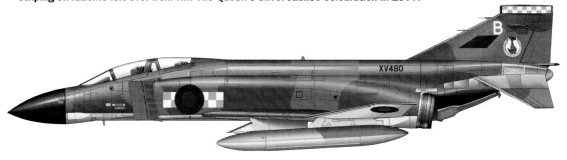

Phantom FGR.2 XV480 of 19 Squadron RAF, Wildenrath, Germany 1982.

F-4E Phantom

The final new production Phantom variant was also produced in the greatest numbers. The YF-4E prototype (62-12200, converted from a YRF-4C which in turn started life as an F-4B) flew on 7 August 1965, followed by the first production F-4E (66-0284) on 30 June 1967, two months after McDonnell and Douglas had merged (to solve the latter's serious cash flow situation) to form the McDonnell Douglas Corporation. Service testing at Nellis AFB, Nevada, began in October 1967 and the 33rd TFW at Eglin was the initial operational user. Vietnam service began in November 1968.

Of the 1,387 F-4Es manufactured at St Louis, 831 went to the USAF and 556 were exported to Israel, Australia, Germany, Greece, Egypt, Iran, Japan, Turkey and South Korea. The last St Louis built F-4E (78-0744 for South Korea) was also the 5,057th and final Phantom from that source and was handed over on 26 October 1979. USAF deliveries had meanwhile ended in December 1976.

The F-4E embodied improvements resulting from lessons learned in combat, the most distinctive of which was the incorporation of a 20mm Vulcan M61 rotary cannon under the lengthened nose. As USAF fighter ace, Colonel Robin Olds, once said: "A fighter without a gun.... is like an airplane without a wing".

Even though earlier Phantoms were capable of carrying an external gun pod, this were far from perfect as it was subject to operational limitations and suffered from shot dispersion caused by the pylon on which it was mounted flexing during firing. Using missiles only, Phantoms had been successful in numerous air to air combats in Vietnam, but many opportunities were missed due to the lack of a fixed gun.

The rules of engagement in Vietnam were that positive visual identification of a target had to be made before firing, and that requirement often meant the target aircraft was too close for the Sparrow or Sidewinder missiles to be used.

The gun (with 640 rounds of ammunition) was mounted below the nose. In Vietnam, F-4Es were responsible for downing 23 MiG-19s and -21s. Of those, six fell to the gun alone, one to a combination of gun and missile, and the remainder to missiles. The first kill (a MiG-19 by Sparrow missile) was to the 35th TFS's Lt Col L L Beckers and Capt J F Huwe on 23 May 1972.

May 1988, and '30 Years of Phabulous Phantoms' is celebrated on this early production F-4E (68-0336) operated by the 131st Tactical Fighter Wing, Missouri Air National Guard.

This head on view of an F-4E shows the leading edge slats fitted to the aircraft from mid 1972. The slats significantly improved the Phantom's turning ability but came too late to see service in Vietnam.

Other changes included the introduction of the more capable, lighter, smaller, reliable and completely solid state Westinghouse APQ-120 radar; a seventh fuselage fuel cell; improved weapons management; the slotted stabilator of the F-4J (see below); and more powerful J79-GE-17 engines, each producing 11,870lb (52.8kN) dry thrust and 17,900lb (79.6kN) thrust with afterburner.

The second major change introduced on the F-4E came well into the model's production life but was subsequently retrofitted to earlier aircraft. Leading edge wing slats (often called 'manoeuvring slats') were fitted to new production aircraft from mid 1972, too late to see service in Vietnam. Their fitting resulted from the various Agile Eagle programmes starting in 1969 and originally intended to enhance the manoeuvrability of the F-15 Eagle. Several configurations were tested and the 756th F-4E (71-0237) was the first one built from new with the definitive arrangement. Again, their fitting was a result of combat experience.

Vietnam proved yet again that dogfights tend to get lower, slower and tighter as they progress and combat against the more nimble MiGs often resulted in Phantom pilots pulling too tight at low altitudes with the inevitable stall/spin into the ground.

The slats improved the Phantom's turning ability considerably and increased the margin of safety. At Mach 0.9 a slatted F-4E could complete a 180 degree turn of 0.7nm (1.3km) radius in 14 seconds, whereas an unslatted example would be 0.4nm (740m) behind and 0.2nm (370m) outside, a considerable distance. The fitting of slats to the F-4E was not a simple matter and required what was virtually a rebuild of the wings.

Other improvements introduced to the F-4E during its production life included fitting an improved brake anti skid system, gunsight camera, upgraded avionics, self sealing fuel tanks (belatedly) which reduced internal capacity by 7 per cent; a wraparound polycarbonate/acrylic windscreen, low smoke J79-GE-17C/E engines, a TV camera based target identification system and a lengthened gun blast diffuser under the nose which cured an ongoing flameout problem when the M61 was fired by modifying the gas ejection direction and cooling and decelerating the blast.

RF-4E: A tactical reconnaissance version for export only (150 built for West Germany, Greece, Iran, Israel, Japan and Turkey) which combined the F-4E's basic airframe (with unslatted wings) and engines with the RF-4C's equipment fit but with some of the more security 'sensitive' items deleted. The first RF-4E (69-7748) flew on 15 September 1970 and Luftwaffe service began in January 1971. German industry participated in the RF-4E programme, providing major airframe components for it, the Luftwaffe's F-4Fs (see below) and other Phantoms.

Vietnam experience showed that even supersonic fighters needed a gun as well as missile armament, the F-4E introducing a General Electric M61 rotary cannon under the nose. The F-4E entered service in late 1967 and went on to be the most produced and exported of all the Phantom models.

The tactical reconnaissance RF-4E was for export only, built for West Germany, Greece, Iran, Israel, Japan and Turkey from late 1970. 75-0419 was destined for Israel.

A February 1978 view of the McDonnell Douglas production line at St Louis with some of the last F-4Es visible. The 5,000th Phantom is second from the bottom and F-15 Eagles are in the background.

F-4E(F): Original proposals to West Germany were based on a lightweight single seater Phantom called the F-4E(F) with simplified systems and structures and heavily restricted ordnance capability. It was for Germany's Phantoms that the wing slats were first mooted.

F-4EJ: The only country to manufacture and assemble Phantoms outside the USA was Japan, which in addition to the two initial aircraft supplied direct from McDonnell Douglas in 1971 had 138 F-4EJs built by Mitsubishi and delivered between 1972 and 20 May 1981 when the last new Phantom from any source was handed over to the Japanese Air Self Defence Force. Of the 138 Mitsubishi built F-4EJs, the first 26 were manufactured by McDonnell Douglas but assembled by the Japanese company; the remainder were of local production.

RF-4EJ: Despite the 'E' in the designation, the 14 reconnaissance Phantoms delivered to the JASDF differed only in detail to the RF-4C. All were built in the USA by McDonnell, the first example flying on 26 November 1974.

F-4E(S): A designation ('S' for 'Special') covering three unslatted F-4Es (69-7567, 7570 and 7576) converted for high speed reconnaissance duties before delivery to the Israeli Defence Force. The basis of the conversion was the installation of the very large HIAC-1 high altitude optical camera in a slightly reshaped and lengthened nose, the camera replacing the radar previously fitted. A highly secret project, the conversions were performed by General Dynamics and the first one flown on 20 December 1975.

F-4F: The F-4F for the West German Luftwaffe was similar to the F-4E but was some 3,300lb (1,497kg) lighter, lacking stabilator slots, some of the classified US electronics, one fuselage fuel cell and Sparrow missile

The Luftwaffe's F-4Fs had many components (including airframe assemblies and engines) manufactured in West Germany but the aircraft were assembled and flight tested by McDonnell Douglas in the USA. 37+01 (below) was the first F-4F, recording its maiden flight in May 1973.

capability. Major airframe components and the engines were manufactured in Germany (by MBB and MTU, respectively) and shipped to St Louis where final assembly and flight testing of the aircraft took place.

The first F-4F flew on 16 May 1973 and the last was delivered in April 1976. Subsequent upgrades in the early 1980s include the fitting of a digital weapons computer and improved ECM and cockpit displays plus the ability to carry new weapons such as the AGM-65 Maverick air-to-ground missile and the later generation AIM-9L Sidewinder AAM. The more recent F-4F ICE (Improved Combat Efficiency) upgrade is described later.

F-4G Wild Weasel: An operationally important F-4E conversion, the F-4G 'Advanced Wild Weasel' was an electronic countermeasures aircraft for the suppression of enemy weapons radar guidance systems, particularly those associated with air-to-surface missiles. Originally designated EF-4E, the Wild Weasel concept was developed during the Vietnam War and successfully tested by small numbers of EF-4C and EF-4D aircraft.

The idea revolved around the aircraft carrying an array of electronic 'black boxes' to detect, identify, locate and suppress hostile radar along with weaponry to destroy it. In the F-4G's case, precision guided air-to-surface missiles such as the AGM-45 Shrike, AGM-78 Standard anti radiation missile, AGM-88 HARM (High speed Anti Radiation Missile) and AGM-65 Maverick were carried. Although the F-4E's gun and capability to carry conventional strike weapons was removed, provision was made for the carriage of Sidewinder air-to-air missiles for self defence.

The heart of the F-4G was its APR-38 radar and missile detection and launch homing system with most of its antennae and receivers grouped under the nose in a fairing similar in shape to that which previously housed the F-4E's M61 cannon. While the F-4G could carry out both the search and destroy phases of its mission, it was often used as part of a larger force within which it located and suppressed enemy radar while other aircraft destroyed it.

Bristling with large numbers of sensors, jammers and other electronic devices (plus effective weapons), the F-4G proved to be a success in the 1991 Gulf War, nullifying Iraqi defences with HARM missiles ahead of the initial air strikes of the battle.

F-4G conversions totalled 116 aircraft, the first of them (69-7254) flying on 6 December 1975 and the last in 1981. The aircraft had its capabilities upgraded over the years and plans to retire it from USAF service in the early 1990s were temporarily reversed, but the last operational unit (the 561st FS) was deactivated in 1996.

QF-4E/G: A current programme in 2000 to meet a USAF has a requirement for up to 300 QF-4E/G drones, the conversions being undertaken by Tracor Flight Systems.

Most of Japan's 140 F-4EJs were assembled or manufactured under licence by Mitsubishi but the first two were supplied from St Louis. 17-8301 was the first of them, flown in January 1971.

McDONNELL DOUGLAS F-4E PHANTOM

Powerplants: Two General Electric J79-GE-17A axial flow turbojets each rated at 11,870lb (52.8kN) dry thrust and 17,900lb (79.6kN) with afterburner. Internal fuel capacity 1,855-1,994 USgal (7,022-7,548 l) in seven fuselage bladder tanks and integral wing tanks; provision for one 600USgal (2,271 l) underfuselage drop tank and two 370 USgal (1,400 l) underwing drop tanks.

Dimensions: Wing span 38ft 7½ in (11.77m); length 63ft 0in (19.20m); height 16ft 5in (5.00m); wheel track 17ft 9in (5.41m); wing area 530sq ft (49.2m²); aspect ratio 2.82:1; centre wing dihedral nil, outer wing dihedral 12 deg; sweep back 45 deg.

Weights: Basic empty 31,853lb (14,448kg); normal takeoff 58,000lb (26,309kg), max takeoff 61,795lb (28,030kg); 'g' limits 7.75 subsonic and 5.93 supersonic at 58,000lb (26,309kg).

Armament: One General Electric M61A-1 20mm multi barrel cannon under nose with 640 rounds; four Sparrow radar guided AAMs semi recessed under fuselage; one centreline and four underwing pylons capable of carrying up to 16,000lb (7,257kg) of stores including drop tanks, Sidewinder or Falcon AAMs, conventional and nuclear bombs, mines, fire bombs, cluster bombs, practice bombs, flares, rocket packs, ECM pods, towed targets, cameras pods, spray tanks and Walleye or Shrike air-to-surface missiles.

Performance: Max speed Mach 2.17 (1,244kt/2,306km/h) at 36,000ft (10,970m), Mach 1.2 (790kt/1,464km/h) at 1,000ft (300m); max initial climb (max weight-clean) 6,170-49,800ft (1,880-15,180)m/min; service ceiling (max weight-clean) 28,100-58,750ft (8,565-17,905m); tactical radius (eight AAMs and centreline external tank) 170nm (315km); tactical radius (four AAMs, 4,000lb/1,814kg bombs, external tanks) 570nm (1,056km); ferry range (external fuel) 1,718nm (3,184km) at 500kt (926km/h) at 40,000ft (12,190m).

An F-4G Wild Weasel firing an AGM-88 High Speed Anti-Radiation Missile (HARM) during testing by the 4485th Test Squadron's Detachment 5 based at George AFB, California.

Opposite: converted from the F-4E, the F-4G 'Advanced Wild Weasel' defence suppression aircraft first flew in December 1975 and remained in service until 1996. This F-4G (69-0263) is carrying AGM-45 Shrike, AGM-65 Maverick and AGM-78 Standard air-to-ground missiles.

F-4J Phantom

The second major new production Phantom naval variant, the F-4J was developed as a follow on to the F-4B with increased capability (especially in the ground attack role) and improved takeoff and landing performance through lower approach and rotation speeds.

The first production F-4J (BuAer 153072) flew on 27 May 1966 and deliveries to the US Navy's VF-101 began in December of the same year. The 522nd and last F-4J was delivered in January 1972.

The F-4J introduced several major improvements over the F-4B: power was provided by two J79-GE-10 engines each rated at 17,900lb (79.6kN) thrust with afterburner (similar to the F-4E's -17 but with air rather than cartridge starting); and larger main wheels. Despite the higher weights, the F-4J's 16½ deg drooped ailerons and slotted tailplane covered the requirement of reduced approach speeds, these some 12 knots (22km/h) slower than the F-4B. The standard (unslatted) wing was fitted.

Internally, the fuel was rearranged into seven fuselage tanks plus the integral wing tanks, giving an internal capacity of 1,977 USgal (7,484 litres). Avionics/weapons systems improvements included the installation of a Westinghouse AN/AWG-10 X-band pulse Doppler fire control system in combination with APG-59 radar, the AJB-7 nuclear bombing system and an upgraded electrical system.

The F-4J was used extensively in the Vietnam War bombing campaigns and was the last US aircraft type operating in that theatre, the final US Marine Corps unit departing in August 1973. The US Navy's aerobatic team, the Blue Angels, operated a compliment of seven F-4Js between

The final new production Phantom variant for the US Navy and Marine Corps, the F-4J featured numerous improvements over the F-4B. It was used extensively as a bomber in Vietnam and was the last US military type to operate in that theatre.

1969 and 1973 when operations were suspended following a series of crashes.

F-4J (UK): Britain's Royal Air Force became an F-4J operator from August 1984 when the first of 15 second hand aircraft was delivered, purchased to equip a squadron which replaced a previously United Kingdom based unit which was sent to defend the Falklands Islands following the 1982 skirmish with Argentina. These aircraft were designated F-4J (UK) Phantoms, the obvious FGR.3 designation not officially adopted. They incorporated a small amount of British equipment, the most significant of which was the Skyflash air-to-air missile. Their superior performance to the Spey engined Phantoms in RAF service was noted and the last was retired in January 1991.

DF-4J: Conversion (possibly only one) of an EF-4J (see below) to a drone director aircraft with the controls and transmitter equipment in the rear cockpit.

EF-4J: Two F-4Js converted to high speed targets and threat simulators in 1977 for the training of air defence radar operators and to test the systems.

F-4S: The US Navy's F-4Js were subject to numerous systems/electronics upgrades over the years, but a major structural refurbishment of 248 aircraft resulted in a new designation, F-4S. Modifications include the replacement of the original wing leading edge flaps with manoeuvring slats (from the 48th aircraft), structural strengthening, the fitting of new outer wings, 'smokeless' J79-GE-10B engines, digital AWG-10B radar/weapons control system and many other detailed systems modifications designed to prolong the aircraft's life and improve its effectiveness.

The first F-4S conversion (BuAer 158360) was flown on 22 July 1977 and the last delivered in January 1982. The F-4S was the final Phantom variant in Navy and Marines service, the services retiring them in 1989 and 1990, respectively.

QF-4S: Designation covering a planned drone conversion programme for which only the prototype conversion (BuAer 158358) was completed in 1988.

The old and the new. F-4J Phantom BuAer 153852 of the Naval Air Test Centre formates on its successor in USN/USMC service, the first prototype F/A-18 Hornet. The photograph was taken in March 1979, four months after the Hornet's first flight.

The Spey Phantoms

The only Phantoms not powered by General Electric J79 engines were the 52 Phantom FG.1s (F-4K) and 118 Phantom FGR.2s (F-4M) built for Britain's Royal Navy and Royal Air Force from 1966. Of the 52 F-4Ks, 24 went to the Royal Navy and the remainder to the RAF, while all of the F-4Ms were delivered to the latter.

The decision to purchase Phantoms for the RN and RAF was made in 1965 following the 1964 abandonment of the Hawker P.1154 supersonic V/STOL project which was planned in both naval and land based forms. Cancellation of the P.1154 was one of the first acts of the newly elected British socialist government of Harold Wilson, which subsequently went about attempting to destroy the British aircraft industry.

Although based on the USN's F-4J, the Spey Phantom featured significant differences, not the least of which was the installation of two Rolls-Royce Spey 202/203 turbofans each producing 20,515lb (91.2kN) thrust with afterburner. The decision to fit the Spey was a political one designed to soften the effects of the P.1154 cancellation and the job losses which followed.

A considerable amount of British sourced avionics, instruments, systems and equipment was specified for the same reason, as was the incorporation of British made major airframe components including the rear fuselage and tail by BAC and the outer wings and leading edge flaps by Shorts. About 40 per cent of the Spey Phantom (by value) was of British content.

The new engine installation resulted in substantial structural changes to cope with its different dimensions and a 20 per cent increase in required mass flow. The changes included a new engine bay, wider inlet ducting, a wider fuselage, larger jet nozzles and a reshaped lower rear fuselage. This and the need to redesign the Spey for supersonic flight, high 'g' manoeuvres and to fit it with an afterburner led to very high development costs amortised over a relatively small production run and an airframe/engine marriage which was far from ideal.

The result was a Phantom which although still highly capable, was not without its shortcomings. Compared with its US built counterparts, the Spey Phantom was slower, more expensive, and had an inferior rate of climb and

XT595, the first Phantom YF-4K with Rolls-Royce Spey engines. First flown in June 1966, the aircraft was designated Phantom FG.1 in Royal Navy service. This view shows some of the rear fuselage changes and larger jet pipes made necessary by the larger diameter Spey turbofan.

Phantom FG.1 XV588 of the Royal Navy's No 892 Squadron aboard HMS *Ark Royal*. Note the double extended nosewheel leg, designed to provide a greater angle of attack for launch from the relatively small carrier.

ceiling. On the positive side, the more fuel efficient Spey turbofans did provide improved range and endurance.

Orders for the Spey Phantom were placed in 1965-66, initially covering two prototype and 59 production F-4K/FG.1s for the Royal Navy and two prototype and 150 production F-4M/FGR.2s for the RAF. Due to the British Government's insistence on fixed price contracts (and the much larger than expected development cost of the programme) the total purchase was reduced to only 52 F-4Ks and 118 F-4Ms, resulting in a very high unit cost.

F-4K Phantom FG.1: The Spey Phantom developed in a remarkably short time, with the first of two YF-4K prototypes (XT595) flying the for the first time on 27 June 1966. This was the 1,449[th] Phantom to leave McDonnell's St Louis production line.

The first production F-4K (XT597) flew on 2 November 1966 and the first operational RN Fleet Air Arm unit commissioned on the Phantom was 892 Squadron at Yeovilton (later embarked on HMS *Ark Royal*), the only front line unit to operate type. The last example was delivered to the RN on 21 November 1969.

Features of the F-4K included Ferranti AWG-11 radar fire control system (the USA's AWG-10 built under licence) housed in a folding radome to reduce overall length so the aircraft could be accommodated on the relatively small British carriers, strengthened undercarriage to cope with higher specified sink rates on landing, and a strengthened arrester hook.

In order cope with the smaller decks of British carriers, landing speeds had to be kept to a minimum, 16½ deg drooped ailerons were fitted along with larger leading edge flaps and stabilator slots.

To achieve a greater angle of attack on launch, the F-4K featured a double extendable (to 40in/1.02m) nosewheel leg, giving the aircraft a very distinctive nose up/tail down stance when sitting on the ship's deck awaiting the catapult to send it away.

With the end of fixed wing flying from conventional aircraft carriers by the RN in 1978, the Senior Service's surviving F-4Ks were transferred to the RAF.

F-4M Phantom FGR.2: The first of two YF-4M prototypes for the RAF (XT852) was flown on 17 February 1967 and the first production F-4M (XT891) on 26 December 1967. Deliveries began in August 1968 and the first operational squadron to receive the aircraft was No 6 in May 1969. The final example was delivered on 29 October 1969.

The F-4M Phantom FGR.2 was a true multirole aircraft lacking some of the F-4K's naval features (provision for catapult launch, extended nose leg, aileron droop) but retaining folding wings and the arrester hook and incorporated larger low pressure tyres and anti-skid brakes. AWG-12 radar/fire control system (interfaced with a Ferranti inertial nav/attack system), more complete ECM equipment, a standard non slatted stabilator, upgraded avionics and the ability to carry either an EMI reconnaissance or SUU-23A

The first of two YF-4M Phantom prototypes for the RAF (XT852) outside its place of birth at the time of its first flight in February 1967. Deliveries of production Phantom FGR.2s began in August 1968.

gun pod on the centreline (the latter containing a 20mm M61 Vulcan rotary
cannon) were other features. Some F-4Ms were fitted with dual controls for
conversion training.

In the air defence role, the RAF's Phantoms were armed with AIM-7 Sparrow or AIM-9 Sidewinder missiles, with the Sparrow subsequently replaced by
the BAe Dynamics Sky Flash. The last RAF Phantoms were retired in 1992,
replaced by Tornados.

McDONNELL DOUGLAS F-4M PHANTOM FGR.2

Powerplants: Two 12,550lb (55.8kN) dry thrust or 20,515lb
(91.2kN) with afterburner Rolls-Royce RB.168-25R Spey Mk.202/
203 turbofans. Internal fuel capacity 1,977 USgal (7,484 l); max
fuel with external tanks 3,318 USgal (12,560 l).

Dimensions: Wing span 38ft 5in (11.71m); length 57ft 11in
(17.65m); height 16ft 5in (5.00m); wing area 530sq ft (49.2m^2).

Weights: Approximate empty 30,000lb (13,608kg); normal
loaded 49,000lb (22,226kg); max takeoff 58,000lb (26,309kg).

Armament: Air defence - one 20mm M61A1 Vulcan rotary cannon
in centreline pod, four AIM-7E Sparrow III or BAe Sky Skyflash and
four AIM-9D/L Sidewinder air-to-air missiles. Strike - various
external ordnance including 11 1,000lb (454kg) Mk.14 bombs,
10 Matra pods (each with 18 68mm rockets), Martel air-to-surface
missiles, etc.

Performance: Max speed Mach 1.2 (790kt/1,463km/h) at 1,000ft
(305m), Mach 1.9 (1,090kt/2,020km/h) at 36,000ft (10,970m);
tactical radius with six 1,000lb (454kg) bombs and two drop tanks
(hi-lo-hi mission) 478nm (885km) or (lo-lo-hi mission) 330nm
(612km); ferry range with max external fuel 2,172nm (4,024km).

Phantom Upgrades

The Phantom has been subject to modification and upgrading through out its life, and even at the beginning of the 21st century the aircraft is looking to at least another decade of front line service with some nations. The following summarises the major Phantom upgrade programmes.

IAI Phantom 2000: Israel began looking at extending the lives of its large fleet of F-4Es to beyond 2000 in the mid 1980s, this resulting in two programmes developed by Israel Aircraft Industries (IAI), the Phantom 2000 (or *Kurnass* 2000) structural and systems upgrade and the re-engined Super Phantom. *Kurnass* is the F-4E's nickname in Israeli service, meaning 'sledge-hammer'.

The Phantom 2000 upgrade involves complete rewiring, strengthened and in some cases replaced structural components and skinning, reinforced fuel cells to cure leaking problems, rerouted hydraulic lines, the installation of built in test equipment (BITE), a modernised and updated cockpit, APG-76 multimode high resolution radar, head up display (HUD), multifunction electronic displays for both crewmen, digital weapons delivery and navigation system with hands on throttle and stick (HOTAS), improved electronic countermeasures capability and an integrated communications/navigation systems. An Elbit mission computer is at the core of the avionics suite.

The first Phantom 2000 flew on 11 August 1987 and deliveries to the Israeli Air Force began in April 1989. The IAF programme was completed in 1994 after about 55 conversions had been performed.

IAI has offered the Phantom 2000 to the export market, Turkey selecting it in 1996 in a $US632m programme covering 54 aircraft. The first 32 conversions were performed in Israel by IAI and the remainder in Turkey from kits supplied by IAI. The first Turkish conversion was delivered in March 1999.

IAI Super Phantom: This re-engined F-4E began as a test bed programme for the 20,620lb (91.7kN) thrust with afterburner Pratt & Whitney PW1120 turbofan. This had been selected for the indigenous IAI Lavi fighter and was subsequently planned to be offered as part of the Phantom 2000 upgrade. A prototype with a PW1120 in the starboard nacelle only first

The first of 54 Israel Aircraft Industries Phantom 2000 upgrades ordered by Turkey. 73-1025 (its original USAF serial number) was redelivered to the *Turk Hava Kuvvetleri* in March 1999.

flew on 30 July 1986, and was followed by the first flight with two engines installed on 24 April 1987. The new engines endowed the F-4E with substantially improved speed, climb, acceleration and turn performance but cancellation of the Lavi effectively ended the Super Phantom programme.

F-4F ICE: The Luftwaffe initiated its *Kampfwertsteigerung* (KWS) or Improved Combat Efficiency (ICE) F-4F programme in 1983, the upgrade revolving around replacing the original Westinghouse APQ-120 radar with the digital, multimode Hughes (now Raytheon) APG-65 radar built under licence in Germany; installing Hughes AIM-120 advanced medium range air-to-air missile (AMRAAM) capability; a digital fire control computer; digital air data computer; inertial navigation system; digital databus; new cockpit displays; new IFF system and improved jamming resistance.

Prime contractor was the Military Aircraft Division of MBB (now ChryslerDaimler Aerospace - DASA) and the first fully modified F-4F ICE was flown in May 1990. The first production conversion was delivered in April 1992 and the 110th and last in October 1996.

A variation of the ICE configuration was selected by Greece in 1997 under its *Peace Icarus 2000* programme to upgrade 38 F-4Es, combining the APG-65 radar with an Elbit modular multirole computer, integrated GPS/INS, new avionics, IFF, air data computer, HUD, colour cockpit displays and some structural modifications. The first conversion flew in May 1999.

Mitsubishi F-4EJ Kai: A major weapons and avionics upgrade of the JASDF's Mitsubishi built F-4EJ fleet was initiated soon after the last example was delivered in May 1981 under the designation F-4EJ Kai. Initially covering 100 aircraft but reduced to 90 due to attrition, the upgrade included a new fire control/radar system (the Westinghouse APG-66J with look down/shoot down capability), INS, HUD, radar warning receiver and the ability to carry ASM-1/2 anti shipping missiles and subsequently, the Mitsubishi MM-3 air-to-air missile.

The F-4EJ Kai prototype first flew on 17 July 1984 and deliveries began the following December. In addition, 17 F-4EJs were converted to RF-4EJ Kai standards with APQ-172 forward looking radar and an electronic intelligence gathering (Elint) pod. A further 14 existing RF-4EJs were also converted to Kai configuration.

Ninety F-4EJ Kai upgrade conversions were performed for the Japan Air Self-Defence Force, the first of them flying in July 1984. Some - such as this example - were further modified to RF-4EJ Kai standards.

Phantom Operators

Country	Model	Qty	Dates	Notes
Australia	F-4E	24	1970-73	leased from USAF pending delayed F-111 deliveries; 23 returned
Egypt	F-4E	38	1979-	32 in service 1999
Germany	F-4E	10	1977-	
	F-4F	175	1973-	150 in service 1999, 110 F-4F ICE upgrades
	RF-4E	88	1971-97	
Greece	F-4E	84	1974-	74 in service 1999, 38 ICE variation upgrades
	RF-4E	37	1978-	30 in service 1999, 29 ex Luftwaffe
Iran	F-4D	32	1968-?	probably none in service 1999
	F-4E	177	1971-	approx 30 in service 1999
	RF-4E	16	1971-	6 in service 1999
Israel	RF-4C	2	1970-71	on loan from USAF
	F-4E	204	1969-	122 ex USAF, 97 in service 1999, 55 upgrades
	F-4E (S)	3	1976-	high altitude/high speed reconnaissance conversion
	RF-4E	18	1969-	10 in service 1999
Japan	F-4EJ	140	1971-	107 in service 1999, 90 upgrades
	RF-4EJ	14	1974-	12 in service 1999 plus 17 converted from F-4EJ
Sth Korea	RF-4C	18	1988-	ex USAF, in service 1999
	F-4D	69	1969-	ex USAF, 60 in service 1999
	F-4E	67	1978-	37 new build + 30 ex USAF, 60 in service 1999
Spain	F-4C	40	1971-79	ex USAF
	RF-4C	14	1989-	ex USAF, in service 1999
Turkey	F-4E	185	1974-	72 new build, 113 ex USAF, 165 in service 1999, 52 upgrades
	RF-4E	54	1978-	8 new build, 46 ex Luftwaffe, 39 in service 1999
UK - RN	F-4K	52	1968-78	Spey engines, most to RAF
UK - RAF	F-4M	118	1969-92	Spey engines
	F-4J (UK)	15	1984-92	ex USN
USN/MC	F-4B	825	1961-79	
	F-4G	12	1963-65	converted from F-4B on production line
	F-4J	522	1966-84	
	F-4N	228	1973-85	converted from F-4B
	F-4S	248	1979-91	converted from F-4J
USAF/Air National Guard/Air Force Reserve				
	F-4C	583	1963-89	
	RF-4C	505	1965-95	
	F-4D	793	1966-90	
	F-4E	831	1967-91	Luftwaffe training unit disbanded 1997
	F-4G	116	1976-96	converted from F-4E

The Royal Australian Air Force leased 24 F-4Es between 1970 and 1973, as a temporary measure pending delivery of F-111Cs. Of the 23 survivors returned to the USAF, 21 were converted to F-4G Wild Weasel standards. 69-7214 was one of them.

The first of 88 RF-4E Phantoms supplied to the Luftwaffe from 1971. The last was withdrawn in 1997, most going to Greece and Turkey. 35+01 illustrated here also carries its USAF serial 69-7448.

Greece acquired 84 F-4Es and 37 RF-4Es from 1974 with more than 100 still in service by late 1999. An upgrade programme for 38 of Greece's F-4Es began in the same year.

The Imperial Iranian Air Force was a major Phantom customer from the late 1960s, receiving F-4Ds, F-4Es (as here) and RF-4Es before the fall of the Shah in early 1979. The current Islamic Republic of Iran Air Force still had about 36 F/RF-4Es in service in 1999.

Israel's Phantoms have seen plenty of action since the first F-4Es were delivered in 1969. Deliveries comprised 204 F-4Es, three F-4E(S) high altitude/high speed reconnaissance conversions, 18 RF-4Es and two RF-4Cs on loan from the USAF for a brief period in 1970-71. Israel Aircraft Industries had also developed a major upgrade programme for the Phantom.

A Mitsubishi built F-4EJ (87-8404) of the JASDF's 306th Hikotai with a towed gunnery target mounted under its port wing.

Spain was the only export customer for the F-4C Phantom, receiving 40 ex USAF aircraft from 1971. RF-4Cs from USAF stocks were also delivered from 1989, this version remaining in *Ejercito del* Aire service at the start of the 21st century.

Turkey remains a major Phantom operator in 2000 with about 165 F-4Es and 39 RF-4Es in service including 52 being upgraded to IAI Phantom 2000 standards. This is the first Turkish F-4E (73-1016), delivered new in July 1974.

One of the Royal Navy's Spey powered Phantom FG.1s departs, its undercarriage just retracting. The Spey Phantom required a considerable redesign, resulting in performance penalties compared to the J79 powered versions.

Serial Numbers

US New Build Aircraft

Note: the following table lists all Phantoms built with US military serial numbers including those which were subsequently exported. These are noted after the appropriate entry.

YF4H-1: 142259/142260; total 2.

F4H-1F/F-4A: 143388/143395; 145307/145317; 146817/146821; 148252/148275; total 45.

F-4B Phantom BuAer 148413.

F-4B: 148363/148434; 149403/149474; 150406/150493; 150624/150653; 150993/151021; 151397/151519; 152207/152331; 152965/153070; 153912/153915; total 649.

RF-4B: 151975/151983; 153089/153115; 157342/157351; total 46.

F-4C: 62-12199; 63-7407/63-7713; 64-0654/64-0928; total 583.

YRF-4C: 62-12200/62-12201.

RF-4C: 63-7440/63-7463; 64-0997/64-1085; 65-0818/65-0945; 66-0383/66-0478; 67-0428/67-0469; 68-0548/68-0611; 69-0349/69-0384; 71-0248/71-0259; 72-0145/72-0156; total 503.

F-4B Phantom BuAer 150642.

F-4C Phantom 64-0837.

F-4D Phantom 65-0739.

F-4D: 64-0929/64-0980; 65-0580/65-0801; 66-0226/66-0283; 66-7455/66-7774; 66-8685/66-8825; 67-14869/67-14884 (to Iran); 68-6904/68-6919 (to Iran); total 825.

F-4E: 66-0284/66-0382; 67-0208/67-0398; 68-0303/68-0547 (many to Israel); 69-0236/69-0307 (most to Israel, 4 to Australia); 69-7201/69-7273 (20 to Australia); 69-7286/69-7303; 69-7546/69-7589 (some to Israel); 69-7711/69-7742 (to Iran); 71-0224/71-0247; 71-1070/71-1093; 71-1094/71-1166 (to Iran); 71-1391/71-1402; 71-1779/71-1796 (to Israel); 72-0121/72-0144; 72-0157/72-0168; 72-1407; 72-1476/72-1535 (36 to Greece); 73-1016/73-1055 (to Turkey); 73-1157/73-1204; 73-1519/73-1554 (to Iran); 74-0643/74-0666; 74-1014/74-1061 (24 to Israel); 74-1618/74-1653 (2 to Greece); 75-0222/0257 (to Iran); 75-0628/75-0637 (to W Germany); 76-0493/76-0511 (to S Korea); 77-0277/77–0308 (to Turkey); 77-1743/77-1760 (to Greece); 78-0727/78-0744 (to South Korea); total 1,387.

RF-4E: 69-7448/69-7535 (to W Germany); 69-7590/69-7595 (to Iran); 72-0266/72-0269 (to Iran); 74-1725/74-1736 (to Iran); 75-0418/75-0423 (to Israel); 77-0309/77-0316 (to Turkey); 77-1761/77-1766 (to Greece); 78-0751/78-0754 (to Iran); 78-0788 (to Iran); total 150.

F-4F: 72-1111/72-1285 (to W Germany); total 175.

F-4J: 153071/153088; 153768/153911; 154781/154788; 155504/155580; 155731/155903; 157242/157309; 158346/158379; total 522.

F-4J Phantoms BuAer 155787 and 155792.

Royal Navy/Royal Air Force
F-4K: XT595-XT598; XT857-XT876; XV565-XV592.
F-4M: XT852-XT853; XT891-XT914; XV393-XV442; XV460-XV501.
F-4J (UK): ZE350-ZE364.

Phantom FG.1 XT871.

Japan Air Self-Defence Force
F-4EJ: 17-8301/17-8302; 27-8303/27-8306; 37-8307/37-8323; 47-8324/
47-8352; 57-8353/57-8376; 67-8377/67-8391; 77-8392/77-8403;
87-8404/87-8415; 97-8416/97-8427; 07-8428/07-8436; 17-8437/
17-8440.
RF-4EJ: 47-6901/47-6905; 57-6906/57-6914.

F-4E Phantom 66-0336.